DERBY COUNTY
CHAMPIONS 1974-75

Celebrating the 40th Anniversary of the Rams' Last League Championship

DERBY COUNTY CHAMPIONS 1974-75

by Michael Cockayne

First published in Great Britain in 2004 by
The Breedon Books Publishing Company Limited,
3 The Parker Centre, Derby, DE21 4SZ.

This paperback edition published in Great Britain in 2015 by DB Publishing,
an imprint of JMD Media Ltd

ISBN 978-1-78091-460-2

Printed and bound in the UK by Copytech (UK) Ltd Peterborough

Contents

Complete set of the Championship squad and managements' autographs.

Acknowledgements

It would not have been possible to write this book without the help and advice of a number of people. Firstly, Steve Caron and the staff at Breedon Books – thank you for having the confidence to ask me to undertake the project. Also to Kirsty Matkin and her library staff at the *Derby Evening Telegraph*, and also the staff at the Derby Local Studies Library and the Manchester Central Library.

In mentioning the *Derby Evening Telegraph*, any writer involved with Derby County lives in the shadow of Gerald Mortimer. Over 30 years, Gerald reported, analysed and understood, better than most, everything that went on at the football club. His work remains an inspiration.

A particular thank you also to Roy McFarland and Archie Gemmill, who both gave up their time to contribute interviews of their memories. In writing the match reports, I referred to the work of a number of journalists from the era working for *The Times*, *The Telegraph* and *The Guardian* newspapers – thank you one and all – quality survives the years.

On a personal note, although there are too many friends to mention by name, another Harry Chapin quote has been chosen as a thank you all for the support and encouragement, especially during the tough times:

> And so you and I
> We'll watch our years go by
> We'll watch our sweet dreams fly
> Far away, but maybe someday
>
> I don't know when
> But we will dream again
> And we'll be happy then.

Dreams Go By (Portrait Gallery, 1975)

INTRODUCTION

Pre-season Preparations

On 27 April 1974 Derby County beat Wolverhampton Wanderers 2–0 in the final game of their 1973–74 campaign. The victory secured the Rams a third-place finish in the First Division table behind Leeds United and Liverpool. With Dave Mackay's side qualifying for the 1974–75 UEFA Cup competition, more importantly, it also guaranteed the return of European football to the Baseball Ground. Given the turmoil that had engulfed the club following Brian Clough's departure just six months earlier, it was an overall performance which spoke volumes for Mackay's strength of character and resolve to succeed.

Satisfied by the sense of a job well done, the manager then enjoyed a relaxing break in Majorca with his players. However, within days of returning home, his plans for the upcoming 1974–75 season were shattered by news of a serious injury to his centre-half, Roy McFarland. Along with Colin Todd and David Nish, the Rams skipper had been included in the England squad for the annual Home International championship. Although the trio emerged unscathed from a 2–0 defeat of Wales at Ninian Park on 11 May, McFarland badly damaged his Achilles tendon in the single-goal win over Northern Ireland at Wembley four days later. Unfortunately the initial medical reports, which recommended a six-month absence, proved to be wildly optimistic. McFarland underwent surgery immediately after the game and, after a long period of rehabilitation, which included problems with his other ankle as well, it was April 1975 before he could contemplate a return to first-team action. The early speculation that the Rams captain 'would be fit by Christmas' was central to Mackay's decision not to look for a replacement centre-half. With Rod Thomas, an £80,000 purchase from Swindon Town, already in reserve, he opted instead to entrust Peter Daniel, the very reliable second-team defender, with the job of partnering Todd at the heart of the back four.

The injury to the country's first-choice central defender proved to be just one of the problems faced by England's caretaker manager Joe Mercer. The genial former boss of, most notably, Manchester City, had been asked to take charge of the side for the three home nation fixtures, and the subsequent friendly games against Argentina, East Germany, Bulgaria and Yugoslavia. His temporary appointment came after the Football Association had dispensed with the services of Sir Alf Ramsey – the 1966 World Cup-winning manager being dismissed as a consequence of England's failure to qualify for the 1974 World Cup in Germany. From the outset, Mercer declared an intent to put some fun back into the game. His policy saw both Stan Bowles and Frank Worthington, players regarded as untrustworthy mavericks in the Ramsey era, included in the squad. However, Bowles proved to be frustratingly temperamental. After being substituted in the game against Northern Ireland, the Queen's Park Rangers talisman went missing from the team hotel, and then failed to travel to Glasgow for the championship-deciding encounter with Scotland. As it transpired, the Scots beat Mercer's side 2–0, with, unusually, both of the goals being credited to England defenders: after Mike Pejic had put through the ball into his own net, a shot from Kenny Dalglish was deflected past Peter Shilton by Todd. Although the result meant the two nations shared the championship, to Mercer's credit, the loss at Hampden Park was the only one his side suffered during his seven-match reign. The defeat also marked a fifth and final international cap for Nish. The Rams left-back was forced to pull out of the subsequent England tour games after undergoing emergency stomach surgery on the eve of the squad's departure. However, much to Mackay's relief, his record purchase defender made a full recovery in readiness for the start of the season.

Speculation became reality on 4 July when Don Revie was confirmed as the new full-time England manager. It was reported that the Leeds United supremo was lured to accept the job by a five-year contract, believed to be worth in excess of £20,000 a year. Given his impressive record at Elland Road over the previous decade, it seemed to be a sensible appointment. Under his control the Yorkshire club, winners of the title by five points in the season just finished, had also been champions in 1968–69, and runners-up on five other occasions as well. Those who remained critical of the 46-year-old argued that carpet bowls and bingo sessions – all integral parts of his 'family atmosphere' philosophy at Leeds – would not be readily accepted by the established internationals based with other teams. Before leaving Elland Road, the new England manager made a recommendation to the directors about his successor. In fact Revie was so keen to get the right man, he made personal contact with his target. Just as Sam Longson had done when Clough left the Baseball Ground, he tried to convince Bobby Robson that the time was right to leave Ipswich Town. Although, as Robson states in his autobiography *An Englishman Abroad*, Revie was 'very persuasive', the now Knight and member of the footballing pantheon elected to remain at Portman Road. It was no surprise that Robson's name was frequently linked to high-level job vacancies throughout the early 1970s. Under his management, the unfashionable East Anglian side had finished in the top four in two of the last three seasons: a wonderful achievement for a club whose first priority was to balance the books, on regular attendances of well under 20,000.

Revie's appointment as the new England manager had come in the week that the 1974 World Cup reached its climax. Although Scotland, the only home nation represented, remained unbeaten in their opening group games against Zaire, Yugoslavia and Brazil, they were eliminated from the latter stages as a result of their inability to score more than two goals against the African side. The West Germans, on home soil, reached the final and with goals by Paul Breitner and Gerd Muller overcame Holland 2–1, despite the fact that with players of the calibre of Cruyff, Neeskens, Rep and Krol in their line-up, the Dutch had been strong favourites to win the trophy for the first time in their history. With England having failed to qualify for the tournament, the only consolation, albeit very small, for thousands of fans watching at home was the fact that Jack Taylor from Wolverhampton was chosen to referee the final.

After being thwarted in their efforts to bring Robson to Yorkshire, the Leeds board decided to look closer to home to find a new manager. They initially discussed the position with John Giles, their 34-year-old midfield maestro and Eire international, who had been with the club for 11 seasons. Giles was very keen to take the job, but before any details could be finalised his colleague Billy Bremner also demanded an interview. It was a situation which left the directors in a quandary. Not wanting to disrupt the strength of unity that was the bedrock of the Leeds dressing-room, they opted instead to seek an outside candidate, and as a consequence the manager's job was advertised in the national press on 9 July. Within days of the vacancy appearing, Clough's name was being widely touted around as a possible option. The former Rams manager was at the time employed, along with Peter Taylor, by Third Division Brighton and Hove Albion. Although Taylor was happy with life on the south coast, Clough yearned for a return to the big time, preferably at a club within daily travelling distance of his Derby base, where his wife and children had remained. On Sunday 21 July, Manny Cussins, the Leeds chairman, travelled to Brighton and met Clough, who had returned at short notice from a holiday in Majorca, in a local hotel. Once a deal had been finalised, Leeds announced that their new manager would commence a four-year contract on the last day of the month.

Not even the most idealistic of observers would have described the pairing of Brian Clough with Leeds United as potentially a marriage made in heaven. Simply based on the Rams results against the Yorkshire side during Clough's six years at the Baseball Ground – just two victories in 11 League and Cup games, they had certainly become his bogey team, and Revie his *bête noire*. The personal conflict between the duo ran much deeper than merely the outcome of matches between their respective clubs. Clough envied Revie's success, and he despised the methodology behind it. In a vitriolic outburst less than 12 months earlier, he had used his column in the *Sunday Express* to demand action. As a punishment for their tactics, Clough had suggested that Leeds should be expelled from the top flight and their manager given a substantial fine. On the face of it, the newly appointed Elland Road boss needed to embark on a substantial bridge-building exercise. However, rather than undertake any such action, Clough instead adopted an ill thought out approach from the outset. Without the influential Taylor alongside him, he used the initial team meeting to totally extinguish any lingering enthusiasm that the Leeds players may have held for him. In the most basic of terms, the room full of senior internationals were individually lambasted, and informed that their achievements had been based on a cheating approach as opposed to ability. Before a ball had been kicked in anger, Clough found himself virtually without a dressing-room friend. The only individual seemingly unaffected by the outrageous denigration was Allan Clarke – a hugely talented forward who regularly demonstrated the same arrogant and self-centred approach to goalscoring that Clough himself had displayed at the height of his own playing career.

In an attempt to rectify the situation, Clough convinced Jimmy Gordon to rejoin him. The respected trainer of the Rams 1972 championship-winning side replaced Les Cocker, who had followed Revie into the England set up. The signing of Duncan McKenzie from Nottingham Forest, for a club record £250,000, soon followed, but when Leeds subsequently made a poor start to the season, Clough was already living on borrowed time. Immediately after a first-day defeat against Stoke City, he moved quickly to sign John O'Hare and John McGovern for a joint fee of £125,000. Although both players had given the Rams superb service over the years, they had in recent times lost their automatic places in the line-up. Striker O'Hare, scorer of 81 goals in 308 appearances, had been replaced by Roger Davies, while McGovern, with 237 games to his name, had seen Steve Powell and then Bruce Rioch, Mackay's £200,000

An inspired signing. Some of the groundwork for the Rams' Championship glory was put in back in February 1974 when Dave Mackay signed Bruce Rioch from Aston Villa for £200,000. Rioch started quietly but in 1974–75 he scored 20 goals in all competitions and was absolutely vital in Derby's title success.

signing from Aston Villa, replace him in midfield. As the Yorkshire side continued to struggle, all three of the new men found life at Elland Road difficult, their abilities not being fully recognised, either in the dressing room or on the terraces. In the end Clough's appointment lasted for the ridiculously short time of 43 days. Unlike a year earlier at the Baseball Ground, second time around there was no angry resignation. The Leeds directors terminated his contract and replaced him with Jimmy Armfield. It was a move which earned the departing manager a sum in excess of £90,000 in compensation.

Derby had also tried to sign McKenzie after his fall out and transfer listing at Forest. Mackay offered around £200,000 for the 24-year-old striker, who had sprung to prominence in the previous season. Although Forest had finished in seventh place in the Second Division, McKenzie had netted 26 goals – a tally sufficient to earn him top position in the divisional scoring charts. Bizarrely, under Mackay's earlier management of Forest, the Grimsby-born forward had been loaned out to Fourth Division Peterborough United for short spells in both 1970 and 1973. With his target installed at Leeds, Mackay quickly turned his attentions elsewhere to bolster the strike force.

Three days before the big kick-off, he snapped up Francis Lee from Manchester City for £100,000. In what was a busy day for the Mancunian club, they added to their squad by acquiring the services of Asa Hartford from West Bromwich Albion for £250,000. Despite the fact that Lee, at 30 years old, was slightly past his peak, he had significantly – just as Mackay had done when arriving at the Baseball Ground as a player – retained an immense enthusiasm for the game. Over seven seasons at Maine Road, he had won League, FA Cup, League Cup and European Cup-Winners' Cup medals. He also held 27 full England caps, and had scored 112 League goals in 249 games. The signing took the Rams' close-season expenditure to a total of around £150,000, Mackay having additionally paid Waterford £30,000 for 24-year-old Tony Macken, and Albion Rovers £10,000 for Jeff King. Both players subsequently found their opportunities at the Baseball Ground limited, although they did offer solid midfield cover as and when required. Lee's arrival also resolved the Rams five-month search for a striker. As well as having bid for McKenzie, they had earlier been linked to Peter Osgood, who subsequently signed for Southampton, and Dennis Tueart, who had arrived at Maine Road from Sunderland.

Mackay was clearly delighted with the signing. 'Francis has strength, power and is an exceptionally brave player,' he told reporters. With the Rams having struggled for goals on their three-game pre-season tour, it seemed that Lee's arrival was perfectly timed. They had netted just one in their games against German side VFL Bochum and Spanish clubs Granada and Malaga – the matches against the latter pair being part of the four-team Malaga tournament, an event that also featured potential UEFA Cup opponents Twente Enschede from Holland. As well as the lack of goals, another downside of the tour games was that Thomas suffered a groin injury, which was considered serious enough for him to return home early for specialist treatment. As Lee settled into his new surroundings, reserve-team striker Andy Rowland, who had not been included in the Rams 17-man tour party, opted to try his luck with Bury in a transfer deal which netted Derby around £7,000.

On 12 July, as the supporters of Leeds contemplated the post-Revie era, over on Merseyside everyone connected with Liverpool was stunned to hear that Bill Shankly was retiring as their manager. The Anfield club announced his decision to retire just a few hours after the signing of Ray Kennedy from Arsenal had been completed for a fee of £180,000. The legendary Scot had taken charge at Liverpool in December 1959 when he replaced Phil Taylor, the three times capped former England midfielder. His total commitment to the job, typified by the famous maxim 'Football isn't a matter of life or death, its much more important', had seen the club transformed, in the words of defender Tommy Smith, 'From a sleeping giant to an awesome football machine'. Shankly certainly left Anfield with his side at its peak. They had trounced Newcastle

United 3–0 in the 1974 FA Cup Final, that success coming just a year after they had won the championship by three points and captured the UEFA Cup as well. At their Annual General Meeting on 26 July, the Liverpool chairman John Smith introduced Bob Paisley, who had arrived at Anfield as a player in 1939, as the new manager. After his 278-game career, interrupted by the war, had ended in 1954, the then 35-year-old joined the backroom staff – firstly as a trainer and then as Shankly's assistant. He was instrumental in the introduction and development of the fabled Anfield Boot Room, the small windowless room where, over the years, the overall strategy of the Merseyside club was devised.

Although Paisley selected the Liverpool side for the 1974 Charity Shield game against Leeds at Wembley on 10 August, Shankly led the team onto the pitch. It was the first sign of many that he was already finding it hard not to be involved at the hub of the club to which he had dedicated his life. The outcome of the traditional seasonal opener, Liverpool winning 6–5 on penalties, paled into insignificance, however, after the dismissal of both Bremner and Kevin Keegan. The duo became the first British players to be sent off at Wembley, their problems being compounded by the throwing off of their shirts as they trooped off. Not surprisingly, the Football Association took a dim view of their actions, and in addition to the statutory three-game ban, both men found themselves subsequently suspended until 30 September and fined £500. Keegan's dismissal certainly completed an eventful summer for the Liverpool and England forward. Having been sent off in a club warm-up game against Kaiserslautern just four days before the Wembley showpiece, Keegan had also made front-page headlines while on tour with England. As the squad flew into Belgrade airport ahead of their friendly game against Yugoslavia, the national captain was detained by security guards. Although, after protests by the team management, he was allowed to rejoin his colleagues, it was clear that a distressed Keegan had been beaten up during his ordeal.

After what had been a remarkable summer, Geoffrey Green in *The*

Times heralded the 'dawn of a golden new age', his comments being largely prompted by the re-emergence of wing play at the World Cup, in addition to the managerial changes. Green further suggested that if the 'wingless wonders' policy that had prevailed at home since 1966 was reversed, the serious decline in attendances and goals might also be halted. On behalf of the Football Association, the eve of the new League campaign was marked by their newly appointed secretary Ted Croker demanding that discipline be improved, his sentiment being reflected by the lengthy suspensions handed to Keegan and Bremner. Transfer activity involving the top

August 1974 and Roger Davies looks forward to the new season. It was to prove his most consistent as a first-team regular at Derby.

teams had also been very brisk during the close season. In addition to the large fee transfers previously mentioned for McKenzie, Hartford and Kennedy, there were other significant moves, for amounts in excess of £150,000, involving the following players:

PLAYER	FROM	TO	FEE
Larry Lloyd	Liverpool	Coventry City	£240,000
David Hay	Celtic	Chelsea	£225,000
Geoff Salmons	Sheffield United	Stoke City	£200,000
Micky Burns	Blackpool	Newcastle United	£170,000
Alfie Conn	Rangers	Tottenham Hotspur	£170,000

Those major deals took the cumulative spending for the first eight months of 1974 to a figure in excess of £3,000,000 – an indication of the changing financial state of the game.

As the first games of the 1974–75 season drew closer, the sports writers penned their thoughts on the outcome of the campaign ahead. Despite the fact that the Rams had boosted their attacking options with the signing of Lee, the long-term absence of McFarland saw them largely disregarded in terms of being potential title contenders. Indeed, the vast majority favoured either Leeds or Liverpool to emerge as the probable champions, the duo both being offered at odds of around 3/1 by the bookmakers – the Rams drifting out to distant 9/1 options. That was, of course, before a ball had been kicked, and Brian Clough was the manager at Elland Road. Meanwhile, at the Baseball Ground, Archie Gemmill was relishing the thought of leading the Rams into action. Recalling his thoughts, it was clear the that even without McFarland, there was an air of confidence among his squad. 'We felt that there was every chance that we could have a good showing. Dave had brought in one or two players; Bruce, Franny and Rod Thomas, so we were pretty well set up, and we felt reasonably happy before the season started.'

What followed proved to be the most tightly contested First Division campaign for many seasons.

CHAPTER ONE

August 1974

17 August 1974
Football League Division One
Everton 0 v Derby County 0

First day point for Rams as Todd catches the eye...

The Rams opened their campaign with an impressive display at Goodison Park. With Peter Daniel deputising for Roy McFarland, they produced a solid defensive performance and comfortably frustrated the Toffees' expensive twin strike force of Joe Royle and Bob Latchford. At the final whistle the visitors fully deserved their first point of the season, and with two consecutive home games to follow, looked set to make a solid start to the campaign.

Although the home side had the majority of the early play, it was not until the 22nd minute that they created a genuine opportunity. Then Royle headed a corner from Dave Clements downwards, but Colin Boulton superbly parried the effort and the danger was cleared. Everton's inability to prise the Rams defence open resulted

The new season kicked off at Goodison Park with a goalless draw against Everton. Francis Lee made his Rams debut and here he brings the ball away from Dave Clements.

in further chances being at a premium, and as a consequence the crowd of 42,193, the largest of the day, were left in a subdued mood for long periods.

In the second half, although Royle did force Boulton into another fine save after 57 minutes, only half chances from Latchford and John Connolly created any significant ripples of concern in the Rams defence. Indeed without creating a great deal of their own, Dave Mackay's side came more into the game after the break, their increasing confidence not being unduly disrupted even when Kevin Hector was forced to limp off in favour of Jeff Bourne. The substitute linked up well with Francis Lee on a couple of occasions, and looked as though he would be a genuine contender for a regular place in the line-up. Lee, who was signed just three days before the big kick-off, also worked hard throughout and showed showed several neat touches.

Latchford did have the ball in the net 12 minutes from time but, to the frustration of the home supporters, his effort came from an offside position. It did, however, at least spur his side on in the final moments, but Daniel and the excellent Colin Todd dispelled the late flurry with a combination of timely tackles and marvellous anticipation. While the Everton manager Billy Bingham was a disappointed man afterwards, Mackay left Merseyside in a satisfied mood. Ironically, for all that the pre-match anticipation had been about the attacking strengths of the respective sides, this was the only game in the First Division to finish scoreless.

Everton: Lawson, Bernard, Seargeant, Clements, Kenyon, Hurst, Buckley, Harvey, Royle, Latchford, Connolly. Substitute: Lyons.

Derby County: Boulton, Webster, Nish, Rioch, Daniel, Todd, Powell, Gemmill, Davies, Hector, Lee. Substitute: Bourne for Hector (54).

Attendance: 42,193
Referee: Mr Reynolds
Post-match positions: n/a

After the game Dave Mackay clarified the situation regarding Kevin Hector. 'He had a knock on his leg', he told reporters, 'and there was no point leaving him on to hobble around and possibly do himself more damage'. Remarkably, it was the first time since 5 September 1970 against Newcastle United that Hector had been withdrawn from a competitive game, testimony indeed to his incredible resilience. Elsewhere on the opening day, in addition to Stoke City's comfortable 3–0 victory over Leeds United, the other most noteworthy performances in the First Division came from Carlisle United and Middles-brough; two of the three promoted teams. The Cumbrians, in the top flight for the first time in their 71-year history, defeated Chelsea 2–0 at Stamford Bridge, while Jack Charlton's 'Boro went one better – goals from Alan Foggon (2) and John Hickton gave them a 3–0 away success against Birmingham City. Somewhat sadly, those encouraging displays did not receive the column inches that they deserved. Manchester United's Second Division fixture at Orient was marred by off-the-pitch violence. Gangs from the so called 'Red Army' of United supporters ran amok in and around Orient's Brisbane Road ground – with, for the record, goals from Willie Morgan and Stewart Houston earning the visitors, relegated from the top flight the previous May, a 2–0 victory.

Interestingly, on a day when six of the 11 games in the First Division ended in away wins, the Ipswich Town manager Bobby Robson, after his side had won by a single goal at Tottenham Hotspur, urged the Football Association to consider awarding an extra point for a victory away from home. Although his idea was not pursued at the time, the principle, of encouraging attacking play, was eventually introduced from the start of the 1981–82 season when teams were awarded three points for a victory. In all, on what was a fine sunny afternoon, Football League attendances totalled 599,470, approximately 43,000 down on the opening Saturday of the 1973–74 campaign. The figures extended a depressing trend which had seen attendances fall each season since 1966–67, the first after England's World Cup triumph at Wembley.

21 August 1974
Football League Division One
Derby County 1 v Coventry City 1

Spoils shared in Baseball Ground stalemate...

Although the Rams gained their second point of the campaign, they only demonstrated anything like their true potential in the final third of the game. With Kevin Hector having recovered from his opening day leg injury, Dave Mackay named the same 11 that had come away from Everton with a scoreless draw. His Coventry counterpart Gordon Milne, meanwhile, gave a debut to Larry Lloyd, a £240,000 eve-of-season purchase from Liverpool. The major boost for the Rams from the fixture was that Francis Lee opened his goalscoring account and looked to be a very shrewd signing.

With the home side slow off the mark, the Sky Blues seized the early initiative. They went ahead in the 20th minute when a poor clearance from Steve Powell fell invitingly to Dennis Mortimer, who lashed a dipping volley inside Colin Boulton's far post. Bruce Rioch, however, replied almost immediately, his arrowed cross shot from a Roger Davies pass producing the first of several impressive saves from the visitors' reserve-team goalkeeper Neil Ramsbottom, who was deputising for the injured Bill Glazier.

The second half opened with the Rams looking far more determined. Lee went close with a drive on the turn, and David Nish put a good effort wide of the post. With the quiet Hector looking to be feeling the effects of his injury, Jeff Bourne was again introduced into the attack just beyond the hour mark. His arrival prompted a spell of pressure that produced the 68th-minute equaliser. A corner kick from Nish was scrambled out, Powell's return shot being turned in from close range by Lee who, not for the first time in the contest, demonstrated his remarkable awareness in front of the net. Once level, Derby pushed forward in search of a winner. Rioch cracked in a free-kick which Ramsbottom grabbed at the second attempt, and then moments later Powell struck a marvellous volley towards the bottom corner, only to be denied by the energetic Coventry shot-stopper. As the minutes ticked by, it was Rioch again who had the best chance to grab a second goal. He was sent clear by a clever pass from Nish, but his powerful shot was too close to the goalkeeper to cause him any real problems.

A share of the points was the fairest of results. The visitors, in comparison to previous years, looked to be an improved team with Lloyd in their defence. That said, their often wayward left-winger Tommy Hutchinson was in the mood to frustrate his teammates with a series of poor passes. As the Rams supporters drifted away they were disappointed not to have seen a victory, but at least their side had fought back well after a shaky opening.

Derby County: Boulton, Webster, Nish, Rioch, Daniel, Todd, Powell, Gemmill, Davies, Hector, Lee. Substitute: Bourne for Hector (62).

Coventry City: Ramsbottom, Hindley, Cattlin, Mortimer, Lloyd, Dugdale, Alderson, Craven, Stein, Cross, Hutchinson. Substitute: Coop for Craven (27).

Attendance: 25,717
Referee: Mr Capey
Post-match positions: Derby 14, Coventry 17

---

24 August 1974
Football League Division One
Derby County 2 v Sheffield United 0

Todd magnificent as Rams achieve first win...

Dave Mackay made just one change to the side that had drawn with Coventry City: Henry Newton replaced knee injury victim Peter Daniel in the heart of the defence. Like the Rams, the visitors had shared the spoils in their two opening contests, but kicked off in the knowledge that their last Baseball Ground victory had come as far back as the 1946–47 campaign. Sadly for the small contingent of Blades supporters, despite the fact that their team matched the Rams for the majority of the contest, they returned to South Yorkshire having failed to witness an improvement on that record.

Derby attacked from the outset and went ahead as early as the fourth minute. After David Nish and Archie Gemmill combined well on the left, the ball reached Kevin Hector, who coolly placed it into the corner of the net. To their credit, the visitors refused to panic and as the half progressed they came decidedly more into the game. In fact they could have equalised when right-back Len Badger struck a fierce shot from a corner kick, but with Colin Boulton beaten, Ron Webster risked life and limb to head the ball to safety. With the England manager Don Revie among the crowd of 23,088, the Rams' failure to control the midfield area meant that Colin Todd was again required to produce another commanding display. Of the midfielders, only the least experienced, Steve Powell, emerged with any real credit: Gemmill and the particularly disappointing Bruce Rioch fell below their standards of the previous season.

The visitors continued to compete well and almost drew level after 75 minutes. Mick Speight thundered in a long-range shot which Boulton tipped over the bar. Much to the annoyance of the United players, Mr Kew, who had chosen to ignore a linesman's flag on the first goal, pointed for a goal kick. On such refereeing decisions games can often be settled, and this one proved to be no exception.

Within two minutes of the restart, Roger Davies secured the Rams' victory. Francis Lee found his path blocked in the penalty area, but eased the ball across to the lanky striker, who finished in spectacular style. Before the end Lee had a chance to make it three. To his frustration, however, after rounding the goalkeeper he allowed Ted Hemsley enough time to get back and block his shot.

The win extended the Rams' unbeaten run to three games, and moved them up to seventh place with four points. They remained two points behind the initial pace setters Carlisle United and Ipswich Town, each of whom had enjoyed a trio of victories.

Derby County: Boulton, Webster, Nish, Rioch, Newton, Todd, Powell, Gemmill, Davies, Hector, Lee. Substitute: Bourne for Rioch (72).

Sheffield United: Brown, Badger, Hemsley, Eddy, Colquhoun, Franks, Woodward, Speight, Cammack, Currie, Field. Substitute: Williams.

Attendance: 23,088
Referee: Mr Kew
Post-match positions: Derby 7, Sheffield United 15

The hooliganism that had blighted the opening day of the season took a turn for the worse on 24 August. The outcome of the Second Division game at Bloomfield Road between Blackpool and Bolton Wanderers paled into insignificance on the announcement that an 18-year-old local man had been stabbed to death during confrontations between the rival supporters. The realisation that, for a minority, aggression was replacing the largely good-natured banter that had existed between fans in the 1960s, produced a frenzy of activity in the media. With the game also becoming increasingly com-mercialised in a rapidly changing society, it was the clearest evidence to date that the long espoused 'Golden Years' of the sport had well and truly come to an end.

West Ham United's 3–2 home defeat by Everton marked Ron Greenwood's last game as team manager. The 52-year-old, who had masterminded the Hammers' FA Cup Final success in 1964, and their European Cup-Winners' Cup triumph the following year, moved into a General Manager role, with his assistant John Lyall taking over the day-to-day team affairs.

As the preparations continued for a round of midweek matches, there was mounting speculation over the future of Burnley's highly rated midfielder Martin Dobson. Although Tottenham seemed favourites to sign the Lancashire-born player, it was Everton who eventually secured his services. The £300,000 they paid for the 26-year-old set a new British record for a straight cash transfer. Coming just six months after the Toffees had splashed out £350,000 on Bob Latchford from Birmingham, a deal which also involved player exchanges, it underlined a determination to emulate the success of their Red counterparts across the divide of Stanley Park. The same could not be said of Burnley, who over the years had only survived by selling their better players. On this occasion, much to the chagrin of the Clarets supporters, the incoming money was used to finance ground improvements at Turf Moor, including the provision of a new stand named after the chairman Bob Lord. In the six years prior to Dobson's departure, Burnley had earned £750,000 in fees: Willie Morgan, Ralph Coates, Steve Kindon, Dave Thomas and Alan West all having departed for amounts in excess of £100,000.

27 August 1974
Football League Division One
Coventry City 1 v Derby County 1

Derby pay the price for missed chances...

Had the Rams been a little more adventurous in their approach to this game, they would have left Highfield Road with two points instead of one. Despite being good value for a half-time lead, Dave Mackay's side sat back, allowed the Sky Blues to claw themselves back into the match, and ultimately conceded a sloppy equaliser. So, just as had been the case at the Baseball Ground a week earlier, the points were shared. It was certainly a scoreline which, given the overall balance of play, pleased Coventry far more than it did the visitors.

With Rod Thomas making his first appearance of the campaign, albeit in the unaccustomed role of centre-half, Derby should have secured an early advantage. Bruce Rioch took the ball past a despairing Larry Lloyd, but then shot wide with just Neil Ramsbottom to beat. The Rams proceeded to stroke the ball around impressively and went ahead with a superb 22nd-minute goal. Colin Todd, in a marvellous vein of early season form, carried forward a pass from Thomas and fed Roger Davies with a defence-splitting pass. Davies, who had netted a good strike against Sheffield United, again kept his composure in front of the net and put his effort into the far corner. Just before the interval, Kevin Hector glanced a shot across the front of goal – but Francis Lee could not manage to get the vital touch that would have almost certainly have made it 2–0. Had the Rams scored at that stage, Coventry's enthusiasm for a fight-back would have been blunted.

Instead, the home side regrouped and attacked from the outset in the second half, their play forcing the visitors backwards. Although Thomas was beaten a few times in the air, Colin Boulton was not required to make anything other than routine saves. Having survived a spell of pressure, Derby inexplicably seemed to assume the game was won, and soon paid the price. In the 70th minute, a moment of confusion in the penalty area allowed Willie Carr, despite a challenge from Ron Webster, to place a shot wide of Boulton. Towards the end Tommy Hutchinson remained the home side's most dangerous player. Despite the fact that the Rams coped with him reasonably well, David Nish – still not 100 percent fit following his close-season hospitalisation – was booked for hacking down the rangy winger.

Coventry City: Ramsbottom, Hindley, Cattlin, Mortimer, Lloyd, Dugdale, Carr, Alderson, Stein, McGuire, Hutchinson. Substitute: Cross.

Derby County: Boulton, Webster, Nish, Rioch, Thomas, Todd, Powell, Gemmill, Davies, Hector, Lee. Substitute: Bourne.

Attendance: 18,586
Referee: Mr Williams
Post-match positions: Derby 4, Coventry 17

Bill Nicholson resigned as the manager of Tottenham on 29 August. The White Hart Lane side, after four straight defeats, had experienced their worst start to a League campaign for 62 years. Nicholson had joined Spurs as a 17-year-old midfielder in 1938, his managerial career with the club beginning when he succeeded Jimmy Anderson 20 years later. Under his control in the 1960s Tottenham, inspired by a certain Dave Mackay, were a remarkable team, their flowing football bringing an avalanche of trophies to North London including the 1960–61 League and FA Cup double.

As the game saluted the achievements of a great manager, one of the top marksmen of the previous decade announced the end of his career. Denis Law, who had scored 171 goals in 309 League appearances for Manchester United between 1962 and 1973, decided to hang up his boots. His last first-class match had been, appropriately given his patriotism, for Scotland against Zaire in the World Cup. It was of course a goal from Law, discarded by United and in the blue of Manchester City, that had helped relegate the Old Trafford side to the Second Division just four months earlier.

The Rams' defeat at White Hart Lane on 31 August (see report) saw them slip down the League table from fourth to 11th – three draws, one victory and one defeat giving them an opening month total of five points. Bob Paisley's Liverpool topped the standings at the end of the month; the Anfield club and their Merseyside rivals Everton were the only two unbeaten sides. Liverpool had moved into first place following their win at Chelsea, with goals from Phil Boersma (2) and Ray Kennedy giving them an easy 3–0 success. Birmingham and Coventry City, with two points apiece, occupied the bottom places, with the Midlands pair, along with promoted Luton Town, being the only teams in the First Division not to have recorded a victory.

31 August 1974
Football League Division One
Tottenham Hotspur 2 v Derby County 0

The Rams slip to another defeat at Tottenham...

Before the start of this contest the Spurs supporters heralded Bill Nicholson with a standing ovation. The warmth of the greeting for the doyen of English managers certainly energised the Tottenham players. In turn, they responded by putting on their best display of the season to date. Not that the Rams would have been relishing their first visit of the campaign to the capital city. With the memorable exception of a 5–3 FA Cup replay victory in 1973, they had been defeated on five of their last six visits to White Hart Lane, and had rarely performed to the best of their abilities.

With Henry Newton replacing Steve Powell, Derby struggled to create anything of worth during the first half. The staleness of their attack and midfield was amply demonstrated by the fact that a determined run and shot from centre-half Peter Daniel was the sum of what they could muster. That said, for all the possession Spurs had, they conjured up few real scoring opportunities; their best chance came when John Pratt forced Colin Boulton into making a tremendous save. The home side eventually went ahead, however, in the 46th minute. Pratt outsmarted Colin Todd and slipped the ball to Ralph Coates, who floated a cross into the penalty area. Jimmy Neighbour was the quickest player to react and he rifled a powerful volley past Boulton. Seconds after the restart Martin Peters nodded home another centre from the constantly dangerous Coates, but this time Mr Crabb had already ruled that Martin Chivers was offside.

The decision did not prove to be costly for the home side. After 56 minutes Neighbour scored his second, with Pratt again being the architect. The Spurs midfielder headed the ball into Neighbour's path and, after leaving Ron Webster trailing in his wake, the Chingford-born winger slipped his shot past an advancing Boulton from a narrow angle. Soon afterwards Peters, denied by the referee's whistle earlier on, almost increased the advantage after a mistake by Daniel. The Rams defender lost the ball to the World Cup-winner on the edge of the penalty area, but Boulton, becoming increasingly active, reacted with a fine one-handed save.

The final whistle came as a blessed relief to a disheartened Derby side. Although they restricted the home side to two goals, only Boulton, Todd and Newton emerged overall with positive contributions. Indeed, Dave Mackay's post-match observation that 'They could have put six past us' summed up perfectly his side's ineptitude.

Tottenham Hotspur: Jennings, Evans, Naylor, Pratt, England, Beal, Neighbour, Perryman, Chivers, Peters, Coates. Substitute: McGrath.

Derby County: Boulton, Webster, Nish, Rioch, Daniel, Todd, Newton, Gemmill, Davies, Hector, Lee. Substitute: Bourne for Lee (59).

Attendance: 20,770
Referee: Mr Crabb

Post-match positions: Derby 11, Spurs 20

Division One – 31 August 1974

		P	W	D	L	GF	GA	PTS
1	Liverpool	5	4	1	0	9	2	9
2	Ipswich Town	5	4	0	1	8	3	8
3	Everton	5	3	2	0	8	5	8
4	Manchester City	5	4	0	1	9	6	8
5	Carlisle United	5	3	1	1	6	2	7
6	Stoke City	5	2	2	1	7	4	6
7	Middlesbrough	5	2	2	1	6	4	6
8	Wolverhampton Wdrs	5	2	2	1	7	6	6
9	Sheffield United	5	2	2	1	8	7	6
10	Newcastle United	5	2	1	2	10	10	5
11	**Derby County**	**5**	**1**	**3**	**1**	**4**	**4**	**5**
12	Queen's Park Rangers	5	1	3	1	4	4	5
13	Chelsea	5	2	1	2	8	10	5
14	Arsenal	5	2	0	3	6	6	4
15	Leicester City	5	1	2	2	7	8	4
16	Burnley	5	1	1	3	8	9	3
17	Luton Town	5	0	3	2	3	6	3
18	West Ham United	5	1	1	3	4	9	3
19	Leeds United	5	1	1	3	3	7	3
20	Tottenham Hotspur	5	1	0	4	3	5	2
21	Birmingham City	5	0	2	3	5	10	2
22	Coventry City	5	0	2	3	5	11	2

PETER DANIEL

FRANCIS LEE

Chapter Two

September

The headlines of early September were dominated by speculation surrounding the managerial vacancy at White Hart Lane. Given the extent and success of his playing career with Tottenham, Dave Mackay was automatically rumoured to be a possible candidate. The Rams boss, however, moved quickly to dismiss stories linking him to the job. On 3 September he was quoted in the *Daily Express* as saying: 'Obviously I have very deep feelings for Spurs, it's a magnificent club. But if they approached me tomorrow the answer would be no. I have no contract here at Derby, but I'm under an obligation to them. I have been at three clubs in four years – Swindon, Forest and Derby – and have not had a full season with any of them.'

Indeed, rather than moving elsewhere, Mackay's thoughts were more on strengthening his squad. When it emerged that Stan Bowles had again been transfer-listed at Queen's Park Rangers, the Rams boss was the first of several to tentatively enquire about his availability. Although he declined to pursue his interest in the controversial Rangers forward, several of the reserve side were allowed to move on from the Baseball Ground during the month. Jim Walker and Tommy Mason were transferred to Brighton and Hove Albion for a joint £25,000 fee, while Belper-born forward John Sims went out on a month's loan to Oxford United. For Walker it was an opportunity to renew his acquaintance with Peter Taylor, manager of Brighton, and the man who had signed him for the Rams as a 20-year-old in 1968. Those departures followed that of Graham Moseley, who had joined Second Division Aston Villa on a month's loan in August, Mackay stipulating, however, that in order not to be cup-tied, the Rams reserve goalkeeper could not participate in the early stages of Villa's League Cup campaign.

Before tackling Newcastle United on 7 September, the Rams' first game of the month was a midweek testimonial fixture in honour of Mick Hopkinson, the popular Ambergate-born player who had spent nine seasons at the Baseball Ground between 1959 and 1968. A strong Derby squad beat an All Star XI 10–3 at Christchurch Meadows, Belper, with the estimated crowd of 4,000 raising £900 for Hopkinson, who after leaving Derby had played for Mansfield Town and Port Vale before a broken leg sadly ended his professional career.

7 September 1974
Football League Division One
Derby County 2 v Newcastle United 2

Lee on target as Rams come from behind to draw...

Although the Rams dropped another point at a gale-battered Baseball Ground, they did at least perform much better than they had done at Tottenham. Dave Mackay named an unchanged side with Henry Newton retaining his place in midfield alongside Archie Gemmill and Bruce Rioch. The visitors included both of their major summer signings; defender Glenn Keeley from Ipswich Town, and forward Michael Burns, valued at £170,000, from Second Division Blackpool. The Tynesiders also named Ilkeston-born and developed John Tudor in their line up.

Facing a wind which made good football difficult, Derby attacked from the outset with Roger Davies looking impressive, the Rams striker twice leaving Keeley shambling behind him. With 10 goals already Newcastle had arrived as the division's top scorers, and against the run of play they went ahead just before the half-hour. Burns hit a free-kick into the penalty area, and the lack of a competitive challenge allowed Malcolm Macdonald to head easily past Colin Boulton. The opener stung the home side into a flurry of activity and David Nish hit the post before the equaliser came in the 40th minute. Colin Todd knocked in a clever pass to Francis Lee, and although the barrel-chested forward was under pressure he slipped the ball into the path of Davies, who blasted his shot into the roof of the net.

The start of the second half was delayed. The roof on the Osmaston stand had taken the worst of the winds, and stewards helped move supporters away to other parts of the ground. Once the game got underway again, the Rams continued to press forward with purpose, Lee having by far his best game of the embryonic season. They were rewarded in the 53rd minute when the former Manchester City man blasted home a free-kick, his drive taking a wicked deflection off the wall, which left the goalkeeper stranded.

To their credit, Newcastle responded well and the hard-working Burns demonstrated his speed when he equalised in the 61st minute. Set free by Tommy Cassidy, the striker – who had netted 53 League goals in 179 games for the Tangerines – beat Ron Webster for pace and slipped the ball past Boulton from an acute angle. It was almost a case of déjà vu in the closing moments. Burns again got clear, but the immaculate Todd got back and cleared the ball for a corner. It was a magnificent piece of defending and characterised his start to the season.

Although Jeff Bourne again came on for Rioch, Mackay's £200,000 signing from Aston Villa in February 1974 did at least come off with the satisfaction of having returned his best display of the campaign.

Derby County: Boulton, Webster, Nish, Rioch, Daniel, Todd, Newton, Gemmill, Davies, Hector, Lee. Substitute: Bourne for Rioch (75).

Newcastle United: McFaul, Nattrass, Clark, Gibb, Keeley, Howard, Burns, Cassidy, Macdonald, Tudor, Hibbitt. Substitute: Smith

Attendance: 21,107

Referee: Mr Hart

Post-match positions: Derby 11, Newcastle United 10

Undoubtedly the most entertaining game of the day was at Anfield, where Liverpool thrashed Tottenham Hotspur 5–2. With Tommy Smith and Emlyn Hughes playing their 500th and 300th games respectively for the Reds, Phil Boersma improved on his brace against Chelsea by netting a hat-trick. It was a result which not only kept Liverpool in pole position, but also provided the ideal tonic for manager Bob Paisley, who had been slightly injured in a car accident a few days before the game. While it was a good day for Boersma, the reverse was definitely the case for John McGovern. Chosen to replace Billy Bremner in the number four shirt for Leeds United against Luton Town, the former Rams midfielder was subjected to a torrent of abuse from sections of the Elland Road crowd. His case was not helped by the fact that Leeds struggled to achieve a 1–1 draw against the side who had only been promoted in May 1974, and had failed to win any of their opening five games. Ipswich Town maintained their impressive start to the season with a single-goal home victory against Everton. In what was a scrappy contest, the East Anglian side took the points with a 29th-minute goal from Clive Woods. With gales affecting most areas of the country, Bobby Robson's post-game instruction to reporters was: 'Don't write a word about this match until you have stood in the centre circle for five minutes'. At the other end of the table, that defeat for Spurs at Anfield left them anchored at the bottom with just two points – one below Coventry City and West Ham United.

The first competitive midweek action of the month saw the Rams drawn against Portsmouth in the second round of the League Cup. Although, as the match report shows, they progressed with ease, several First Division sides found the going much tougher. The holders Wolverhampton Wanderers crashed out 3–1 at home to Second Division Fulham, while at Gresty Road Crewe produced a massive shock as Birmingham City found the team from the bottom division too strong for them. An 89th-minute goal from Peter Lorimer scraped Leeds a 1–1 draw at Third Division Huddersfield Town. It was, however, a scoreline that triggered the end of Brian Clough's Yorkshire sojourn. Forty-eight hours after the game, and despite initial denials to the contrary from Manny Cussins, Clough was fired – the United players having apparently passed a vote of no confidence in their manager of just 43 days. As Clough departed from Leeds, 32-year-old Terry Neill was appointed as the new manager at struggling Tottenham. His arrival at White Hart Lane ended his role as a dual boss, the former Arsenal utility man having been in control of Hull City as well as being the part-time boss of Northern Ireland.

---

11 September 1974
Football League Cup 2nd Round
Portsmouth 1 v Derby County 5

Magnificent Derby stroll to victory...

The final scoreline at Fratton Park did not reveal the true extent of the Rams' domination of this game. Although their critics might speculate that the defeat of a struggling Second Division side by a four-goal margin was nothing special, the reality was that few teams could have competed with Dave Mackay's side. His delight at the performance was summed up by the comment that 'it was the best performance since I became manager'.

Derby again benefited from the advantage of an early goal. After controlling proceedings from the first whistle, they went ahead on 10 minutes when Kevin Hector lashed in a fierce right-foot shot from at least 30 yards out. Roger Davies almost made it 2–0 soon afterwards, but it was Francis Lee who netted the second on the half-hour. With his instincts as quick as ever, Lee picked up a deflected volley from Davies and whipped the ball past David Best from close range.

Any chances of a Pompey revival were extinguished immediately after half-time. Within two minutes of the restart, Bruce Rioch ran unchallenged deep into the Portsmouth half, fed Davies – and was on hand to knock in the centre-forward's low cross from the right. Five minutes later it was 4–0 to the Rams. Lee got clear of his marker and his centre was nonchalantly converted by Hector – his 150th goal for the club. Although Ron Webster was stretchered off after an accidental collision, the Rams' flow was only temporarily disrupted when Peter Marinello, the former Arsenal player, beat Colin Boulton from a dozen yards out. That consolation in the 70th minute only served to drive the visitors on again. Their last goal, however, did not have the quality of its predecessors – in the 81st minute a shot from Lee squirmed in after a deflection from defender Phil Roberts. It could have been more; Hector had one disallowed for offside, and moments before the end Lee forced the increasingly busy Best into another fine save.

Portsmouth, having parted company with their manager John Mortimore, went into the game trying to persuade Sir Alf Ramsay to occupy their vacancy. That bid proved unsuccessful, but even if the former England boss had been in charge it would have altered little. Derby County, for 90 minutes, were simply a joy to watch.

Portsmouth: Best, Roberts, Wilson, Piper, Went, Stephenson, Marinello, Kellard, Davies, Reynolds, Hand. Substitute: Ellis for Davies (45)

Derby County: Boulton, Webster, Nish, Rioch, Daniel, Todd, Powell, Gemmill, Davies, Hector, Lee. Substitute: Newton for Webster (52)

Attendance: 13,582
Referee: Mr Toseland
Post-match positions: n/a

14 September 1974
Football League Division One
Birmingham City 3 v Derby County 2

Rams' rage as decisions go against them...

After the demolition of Portsmouth, Dave Mackay named an unchanged line up for the Rams' visit to St Andrews – Ron Webster reporting no ill effects after being knocked out during the midweek game. There was, however, to be no repeat of the flowing football that had been the basis for the victory on the south coast. Instead a distinctly out-of-sorts Derby side found themselves 3–0 down, albeit after the conversion of two dubiously awarded penalties, after 79 minutes, and only rallied after Birmingham had been reduced to 10 men.

The Rams' play in the opening 20 minutes gave little indication of the capitulation that was to follow. Kevin Hector looked particularly lively on the right-hand side and seemed destined to add to his brace of three days earlier. Things can change quickly though, and once the home side got a grip of midfield they soon took the lead. In the 29th minute, Trevor Francis cleverly deceived David

Colin Todd and Archie Gemmill during the 3–2 defeat at St Andrews. Kenny Burns of the Blues was later to play briefly for the Rams in the 1980s.

Nish, his low cross from the left being converted from close range by Bob Hatton. For the remainder of the half, and again after the interval, Birmingham – desperate for a result after their League Cup debacle – controlled the contest. Howard Kendall, who had arrived in the Midlands with Archie Styles as part of the £350,000 deal that had taken Bob Latchford to Everton, had a magnificent game. In fact it was only after his departure through injury in the 67th minute that the Rams started to make any progress. They prospered largely, however, because the midfielder's exit, the substitute having been already used at half-time, reduced the home side to 10 men.

Three minutes before Kendall's demise, Birmingham went 2–0 ahead with a disputed penalty. Mr Nippard, on his linesman's flag, decided that Roger Davies had handled in the box, and Francis tucked away the resulting spot-kick. If that piece of refereeing upset the visitors, the award of a second penalty in the 79th minute incensed them. Francis got clear, but Peter Daniel seemed to have saved the Rams' blushes with a perfectly timed tackle. This time, Mr Nippard, who was lagging behind play and received no prompt from the touchline, again pointed directly to the penalty spot – Francis netting his second with ease. Colin Todd protested vociferously to the official, and given the referee's overall performance, it was a surprise that the Rams defender was not cautioned.

Trailing by three, at least Mackay's side gave the scoreline some respectability. In the 84th minute Bruce Rioch reduced the arrears when he netted after David Latchford had blocked a shot from Hector. Then three minutes later Davies notched his fourth goal of the campaign with a good run and drive past the goalkeeper. Sadly, it was all a case of too little too late.

Birmingham City: Latchford, Martin, Styles, Kendall, Gallagher, Page, Campbell, Francis, Burns, Hatton, Taylor. Substitute: Hynd for Page (45).

Derby County: Boulton, Webster, Nish, Rioch, Daniel, Todd, Powell, Gemmill, Davies, Hector, Lee. Substitute: Newton for Powell (57).

Attendance: 27,795
Referee: Mr Nippard
Post-match positions: Derby 14, Birmingham 15

18 September 1974
UEFA Cup 1st Round – 1st Leg
Derby County 4 v Servette 1

Rams net four and seem to be safe...

For the first half of this contest, the Rams followed their manager's instructions to the letter. Dave Mackay, obviously not fearing the Swiss part-timers as much as the stronger sides in the competition, had demanded a three-goal advantage ahead of the second leg.

Derby began their UEFA Cup campaign with a 4–1 home win against Servette of Switzerland. Here Colin Boulton punches clear with Henry Newton, Peter Daniel and Colin Todd in attendance and skipper Archie Gemmill watching. The attendance for a top European night, with seven internationals in the Derby line-up, was a paltry 17,716 and shows how times have changed. The Rams could be struggling at the foot of the new Championship and not expect a crowd as low as that these days, whoever the opposition.

However, having comfortably achieved that objective, his players relaxed in the last third of the game – and conceded the goal that might yet make their visit to Geneva on 2 October slightly uncomfortable.

Jeff Bourne replaced Roger Davies in the Rams frontline: Davies serving the first of a three-game suspension for being sent off in the home leg of the infamous 1973 European Cup semi-final against Juventus. Alan Hinton was named amongst the substitutes, his last appearance having been from the bench, against Leeds United on 6 April.

De Blaireville, the Servette goalkeeper, was in action from early on. Although he did well to turn a cross from Ron Webster on to the bar, only 12 minutes had elapsed before he was beaten for the first time. David Nish hit a left-sided free-kick into the penalty area, the defence hesitated – and Kevin Hector nipped in to steer a downward header into the net. As the Rams pushed forward almost incessantly, Francis Lee was only denied when his superbly energetic overhead effort was kicked off the line by Schnyder. It set the tone, however, and six minutes before half-time the long-anticipated second goal duly arrived. Webster centred following a short corner routine, and Peter Daniel ran in to head home. It was the defender's first senior goal for the club on his 142nd appearance. Four minutes later, Lee also got his name on the scoresheet. After taking a pass from Archie Gemmill, the Rams striker turned sharply on the edge of the penalty area and easily beat the goalkeeper with a crisp left-foot shot.

The crowd had barely settled for the second period when Hector struck again. He took a pass from Nish and beat two ambling defenders for sheer speed before tucking away his shot from 18 yards out. It was undoubtedly the goal of the night, a magnificently executed finish. That should have been the signal for the Rams to add even more to their tally. Instead, they sat back on their advantage, the 54th-minute substitution of Hinton for Henry Newton only serving to disrupt their flow rather than enhance it. Not that the returning wide man could be overly criticised, for by the time he came on those around him clearly thought that their work for the night was complete.

As it transpired, the final word belonged to the Swiss. In the 70th minute their impressive Yugoslavian-born forward Petrovic beat Colin Boulton from the edge of the box, the Rams' last line of defence having just before made a sharp save from Riner.

Derby County: Boulton, Webster, Nish, Rioch, Daniel, Todd, Newton, Gemmill, Bourne, Hector, Lee. Substitute: Hinton for Newton (54).

Servette: De Blaireville, Schnyder, Morganegg, Martin, Guyot, Marchi, Pfister, Castella, Riner, Wegmann, Petrovic. Substitutes: Sundermann for Castella (50), Andrey for Sundermann (62).

Attendance: 17,716
Referee: Mr Riga
Post-match positions: n/a

Elsewhere in the European competitions, English clubs produced a mixed set of first-leg results. In the European Cup, Leeds, with Maurice Lindley installed as caretaker manager, overcame FC Zurich 4–1 at Elland Road with Allan Clarke netting a brace. Meanwhile, in the Cup-Winners' Cup, Liverpool completely overwhelmed the Norwegian minnows Strömsgodset. In their 11th season of European play, the Anfield side celebrated with a goal for each year... the 11–0 final scoreline establishing a new club record. With the exception of midfielder Brian Hall, all of the outfield players hit the back of the visitors' net with Boersma and Phil Thompson both scoring twice.

Of the other English teams in the UEFA Cup, only Wolves found themselves outplayed. They crashed 4–1 in Portugal to FC Porto, with John McAlle having the added misfortune to score an own-goal. Although both of the other two games ended in draws, the visitors, with the advantage of away goals, seemed favourites to progress further. At Portman Road, Ipswich shared four goals with the Dutch side Twente Enschede with Brian Talbot and Bryan Hamilton netting the strikes for Bobby Robson's team. Stoke City held the mighty Ajax of Amsterdam to a 1–1 draw at the Victoria Ground, although that scoreline could have been better if their star midfielder Alan Hudson had not been somewhat hampered by injuries sustained in a car crash a few days before the game.

In the domestic games, there was a major shock at Goodison Park. Second Division Aston Villa, managed by Ron Saunders, thrashed Everton 3–0 in a League Cup replay, a trio of second-half goals giving the Midlands side their unexpected victory. Also in the League Cup, West Ham's improved form continued with a 6–0 replay thrashing of Tranmere Rovers, with the widely travelled Bobby Gould netting a hat-trick.

21 September 1974
Football League Division One
Derby County 3 v Burnley 2

Derby hit back in style after Clarets shock...

In the early stages of this contest, Derby County gave the impression that they had celebrated their midweek victory in the UEFA Cup a little too boisterously. They allowed Burnley the freedom of the park and indeed only really shook themselves from a state of lethargy after the visitors had taken the lead. However, if the Rams struggled in the first half, they were, in the words of Clarets manager Jimmy Adamson, 'scintillating' after the interval. That generous accolade was fully deserved. Derby attacked from the restart, took control, and by the final whistle were splendid value for their victory.

Burnley were quick into their stride, their adoption of a hustling approach forcing the home side into several uncharacteristic errors. They deservedly opened their account in the 20th minute when a

Colin Waldron free-kick, from deep inside his own half, was headed past Colin Boulton by Colin Todd – the Rams defender, under challenge from Ray Hankin, intending to clear the ball behind for a corner. Almost immediately after going behind, Henry Newton hit the bar after a neat pass from Francis Lee. It was a sign of the Rams' growing poise. That said, half-time arrived with the Clarets unfortunate not to have doubled their advantage, Boulton having been forced to save well from the physically imposing Hankin – the Burnley striker who had been dismissed for tangling with Gordon McQueen of Leeds United the previous Saturday.

Burnley took the lead in the 20th minute, thanks to a Colin Todd own goal.

The second period saw Derby play their best football of the season. Kevin Hector, playing his 400th game for the club, celebrated the milestone in style with a 46th-minute equaliser. The serial goalscorer volleyed home superbly after Roger Davies had headed on an Archie Gemmill free-kick. Only nine more minutes had passed before Gemmill masterminded the second goal. He sent Lee away down the left wing, and the resulting centre was clearly handled by the retreating Bill Rodaway. Mr Brent pointed to the penalty spot and Bruce Rioch slammed in the kick in vintage Alan Hinton fashion. In the 65th minute it was 3–1. Rioch forced his way clear, looked up and his cross was cleverly diverted past Alan Stevenson by Lee, who again demonstrated an aggression and awareness which frequently forced defenders into errors. To the visitors' indignation, the goal was scored as their winger Leighton James lay injured.

The only reason that the Rams did not increase their lead was down to the acrobatic and desperately overworked Stevenson. The Clarets goalkeeper, the latest in the seemingly unending supply of Chesterfield-born shot-stoppers, produced several fine saves. Another white-shirted player did, however, get his name on the scoresheet before the end. With just moments remaining, a shot from Hankin went past Boulton off the back of Peter Daniel's leg. It was an untidy conclusion to what was an emphatic second half display.

Derby County: Boulton, Webster, Nish, Rioch, Daniel, Todd, Newton, Gemmill, Davies, Hector, Lee. Substitute: Bourne.

Burnley: Stevenson, Newton, Brennan, Ingham, Waldron, Rodaway, Noble, Hankin, Fletcher, Collins, James. Substitute: Flynn for James (65).

Attendance: 21,377
Referee: Mr Brent

Post-match positions: Derby 10, Burnley 12

The fact that Peter Daniel was able to step in and replace England's first-choice centre-half surprised many, but Roy McFarland certainly had no doubts about the ability of his deputy:

'When Brian Clough and Peter Taylor made a lot of changes in the first couple of seasons, Peter Daniel was there and he saw it through. Although he was classed as a reserve-team player, Peter knew the system at Derby and was used to the players. He trained with them and was entrenched in Derby County and the progress made under Brian, so it was easy for him to slot in. It was a big, maybe hard act to follow, not speaking highly of myself – but I'd been a regular in the side. For Peter to slot in was typical. He was a very likeable lad, a great boy in the dressing room, and just got on with it. Peter stayed because he had qualities. He would stick his head there, stick his leg or body there, he was a very genuine player. The one thing that Cloughie always admired in his players was being genuine – either if you had the ball, or if you didn't. Peter was a very solid defender. Maybe he was a little bit in the mould of Paul Madeley at Leeds, the man that was always there and ready to slot in. Without any doubt Peter had a tremendous season.'

On the day following the Burnley game, 81 of the country's top players met Don Revie at the Piccadilly Hotel in Manchester for what was dubbed by the tabloids as a 'talk-in'. The England manager used the session to announce standards for dress and behaviour, as well as calling for a review of international match fees. Under his proposals, England players would receive £200 for a victory and £100 for a draw – those amounts being in addition to the current match fee of £100. Revie also suggested that success in a major championship should attract a one-off bonus of £6,000. To gauge the value of the incentives that the new manager was proposing, they came at a time when Liverpool, one of the top-paying teams, were rewarding their squad with an annual salary of around £15,000. The Rams were represented at the meeting by McFarland, David Nish, Kevin Hector and Steve Powell, Colin Todd having been allowed to remain in Derby to receive treatment for a groin injury.

25 September 1974
Football League Division One
Derby County 4 v Chelsea 1

Easy for Rams as Daniel scores again...

The crisis of confidence surrounding Chelsea deepened after their performance at the Baseball Ground. The Rams outplayed the Londoners for long periods and emerged as easy winners. More importantly, Dave Mackay's side continued to improve on their already sizeable goal tally – the quartet taking them to 18 in five matches.

Although the initial exchanges were equal, Derby took the lead in the 10th minute. A corner kick was only cleared out as far as Colin Todd, his neat return pass allowing Bruce Rioch to steady himself before firing past John Phillips into the bottom corner of the net. Chelsea did hit back briefly and levelled the contest just four minutes later. Peter Houseman was sent clear and, with the defence anticipating an offside whistle that never came, his perfect centre was headed home by Derby-born forward Ian Hutchinson. After that, however, the Rams took control and added two more first-half goals; surprisingly both scored by defenders. In the 23rd minute, the ruthlessly influential Rioch floated in a free-kick from the right, and Ron Webster ran in to net a fine diving header. It was an effort reminiscent of his headed goal against Manchester City in December 1971. Eleven minutes later it was 3–1. Chelsea again failed to clear a corner properly, their hesitancy resulting in disaster when Peter Daniel rifled home Todd's ball back into the penalty area. It was Daniel's second goal in three games, this from a man who had not previously scored for the club in the previous nine seasons. With the Rams creating opportunities almost at will, there could have been several more goals before the interval; before the third goal came Kevin Hector and Roger Davies had both gone close to increasing the advantage.

The visitors did not improve significantly in the second period. Although Colin Boulton was required to dive smartly to save at the feet of Chris Garland, they otherwise created very little. Instead, as Derby continued to press forward, David Nish also attempted to get in on the goal action – but his superb effort from the edge of the box ricocheted to safety off the top of the bar. The final strike in the 84th minute was a beautiful crafted piece of work. Todd combined elegantly with Francis Lee and, in turn, his pass to Hector was timed perfectly to allow his fellow striker to round Phillips before tapping the ball into the empty net.

It was the best goal of the night and summed up perfectly the Rams' domination. It was a great shame that only just over 22,000 witnessed such an impressive display.

Derby County: Boulton, Webster, Nish, Rioch, Daniel, Todd, Newton, Gemmill, Davies, Hector, Lee. Substitute: Bourne.

Chelsea: Phillips, Locke, Houseman, Hollins, Droy, Harris, Hay, Garland, Cooke, Hutchinson, Sissons. Substitute: Kember.

Attendance: 22,036
Referee: Mr Burns
Post-match positions: Derby 7, Chelsea 15

Following the defeat of Chelsea, the Rams gained a further point from their game at Stoke (see report) on 28 September. Although they dropped one place to eighth as a consequence of the draw, they ended the month just five points behind the leaders Ipswich Town – who themselves were a couple of points ahead of the field despite a 1–0 reversal at Newcastle United. The East Anglians were already proving to be a particularly difficult side to score against. Their defence, inspired by Kevin Beattie, had conceded just six goals in the opening 10 games, and just one at home from five straight victories. In the second half of the month, the East Anglian club had also taken full advantage of Liverpool's sudden loss of form – Bob Paisley's men suffering defeats against Manchester City, Burnley and Sheffield United. It left the Anfield side in third place and eagerly awaiting the return of Kevin Keegan from suspension.

Queen's Park Rangers parted company with their manager on 27 September. After a start to the season that had seen them gain just one victory in nine matches, Gordon Jago resigned his position, a move which which ended a stormy four-year relationship with the Loftus Road chairman Jim Gregory. Jago's departure was the latest upheaval to hit the West London club. Terry Venables, the Rangers captain, had moved to Crystal Palace two weeks earlier, and the already transfer-listed Bowles was again testing the patience of the club by missing several training sessions.

Following the earlier departures of Bill Nicholson at Tottenham and Ron Greenwood at West Ham, Jago became the third London-based manager to be replaced within the opening weeks of the campaign. A glance at the League table after the games of 28 September revealed the malaise affecting the major teams in the capital. The Hammers, in 12th position following a 5–3 win at Burnley, were the highest placed London club. It was a situation which prompted Donald Saunders in the *Daily Telegraph* to predict 'an exceptionally long hard winter in London'. His view was perpetuated by the fact that as well as experiencing falling attendances, Arsenal, Tottenham and the beleaguered Rangers ended the month occupying the bottom three positions.

It was not, however, just the struggling sides who saw their attendances on the decline. While Liverpool could already boast of home gates in excess of 50,000, the majority were experiencing a significant downturn in crowds, a fact reflected as much at the Baseball Ground as anywhere else. Figures for the Rams' opening five League games indicated an average turnout of 22,863, a noticeable reduction from the average of 29,829 that had witnessed the corresponding fixtures of the 1973–74 campaign.

28 September 1974
Football League Division One
Stoke City 1 v Derby County 1

Lee earns Rams another point...

The confidence that the Rams had gained from their victory over Chelsea was again in evidence at the Victoria Ground. Dave Mackay's men knocked the ball around impressively for long periods, their enterprise eventually being rewarded with a goal from Francis Lee 15 minutes from time. Stoke, for whom Geoff Salmons, signed in the close season from Sheffield United, was in outstanding form, had gone ahead just before the half-hour, the Potteries side capitalising on one of a number of free-kicks the visitors conceded.

While Derby were able to name an unchanged line-up, the Stoke manager Tony Waddington was forced to reshuffle his side. Forward John Ritchie had suffered a badly broken leg seven days earlier, so Geoff Hurst was left in the role of a lone striker. While the World Cup-winner, with 202 career League goals before the start of the campaign, worked hard, at 32 he no longer looked to be the top marksman of a few years earlier.

For all of the Rams' neat approach work, it was the home side who created the best early chances. Colin Boulton did well to block an angled shot from Sean Haslegrave, and was then required to save from Jimmy Greenhoff. Stoke did, however, break the deadlock in the 27th minute after a foul on Salmons by Bruce Rioch. Mike Pejic, the England international full-back, floated over a free-kick to the far post where Hurst, despite only managing to get the slightest of touches, squeezed the ball past Boulton. Eight minutes after the goal, Roger Davies wasted a marvellous opportunity to level the contest. Set free by Lee, the Rams striker blasted high over the bar... when it looked easier to score. With both Lee and Davies causing problems for Dennis Smith, Derby could still have had the advantage before the interval. They created another couple of neat moves, and from the second Lee went over in the box, only for Mr Jones, a fair distance from the play, to wave away frantic appeals for a penalty kick.

As the second half wore on, it was the visitors who looked most likely to score. Lee had a goal-bound shot blocked, that chance being followed by an Archie Gemmill first-timer which went just over the bar. The equaliser in the 75th minute was, however, courtesy of an error by the locally born Stoke goalkeeper John Farmer. His fumble of a David Nish header, from a Kevin Hector cross, allowed Lee to nip in and guide the ball home. Stoke rallied and forced a series of late corners, but the Rams, with Todd giving yet another majestic display, held on and deserved their point.

Stoke City: Farmer, Marsh, Pejic, Mahoney, Smith, Dodd, Haslegrave, Greenhoff, Hurst, Hudson, Salmons. Substitute: Robertson.

Derby County: Boulton, Webster, Nish, Rioch, Daniel, Todd, Newton, Gemmill, Davies, Hector, Lee. Substitute: Powell for Rioch (65).

Attendance: 23,589

Referee: Mr Jones

Post-match positions: Derby 8, Stoke City 9

COLIN BOULTON

JEFF BOURNE

Division One – 28 September 1974

		P	W	D	L	GF	GA	PTS
1	Ipswich Town	10	8	0	2	18	6	16
2	Manchester City	10	6	2	2	14	11	14
3	Liverpool	10	6	1	3	17	8	13
4	Everton	10	4	5	1	14	11	13
5	Sheffield United	10	5	3	2	14	14	13
6	Newcastle United	9	5	2	2	16	13	12
7	Middlesbrough	9	4	3	2	12	7	11
8	**Derby County**	**10**	**3**	**5**	**2**	**16**	**13**	**11**
9	Stoke City	10	4	3	3	13	11	11
10	Wolverhampton Wdrs	10	3	5	2	12	11	11
11	Carlisle United	10	4	2	4	8	8	10
12	West Ham United	10	4	1	5	20	18	9
13	Burnley	10	4	1	5	17	18	9
14	Birmingham City	10	3	2	5	12	17	8
15	Coventry City	10	2	4	4	11	17	8
16	Leicester City	9	2	3	4	13	17	7
17	Luton Town	10	1	5	4	11	16	7
18	Chelsea	10	2	3	5	10	18	7
19	Leeds United	9	2	2	5	12	14	6
20	Arsenal	9	2	2	5	9	12	6
21	Tottenham Hotspur	9	3	0	6	11	15	6
22	Queen's Park Rangers	10	1	4	5	8	13	6

Chapter Three

October

Derby through despite early scare...

The Rams duly progressed to the second round of the UEFA Cup on a 6–2 aggregate, Dave Mackay's side netting two second-half goals at the Stade de Charmilles to blunt the enthusiasm of the Swiss part-timers who had taken an early lead.

With Jeff Bourne again replacing the suspended Roger Davies, Derby almost went behind in the opening moments. A free-kick was pushed to Schnyder, who hit a powerful shot past Colin Boulton, only to see David Nish clear the ball off the line. However, just as had been the case at the Baseball Ground two weeks earlier, the Servette defenders soon gave the impression that the speed and reaction time of Kevin Hector was a major concern for them – the Rams striker having, within the first quarter of an hour, a couple of efforts saved by De Blaireville as well as another strike disallowed for offside. The Geneva-based club survived those early threats, and indeed took the lead in the 19th minute. A corner from their player-coach Sundermann was not properly cleared, and Martin arrowed a first-time effort past Boulton. Although both Hector and Peter Daniel responded with shots that went close, the half-time whistle sounded with no further addition to the scoreline; the Rams comfortably holding on to a 4–2 overall advantage.

The final outcome was effectively decided within a minute of the restart. Bruce Rioch knocked in a centre from the right and De Blaireville, demonstrating a Dracula-like reaction to crosses, fumbled the ball to Francis Lee, who gleefully accepted the easiest of chances. The Swiss rallied briefly and Boulton was forced to save twice from Guyot, the second being an excellent finger-tip parry onto the upright. Those opportunities came either side of the Rams' second goal in the 72nd minute. Rioch, showing no signs of the hamstring strain that had threatened his participation, struck a fierce free-kick towards the net, and although the goalkeeper blocked the shot – and a follow up from Bourne – Hector was not to be denied and nodded home the second rebound.

The visitors thus achieved their objective with some considerable ease. The nature of some of the refereeing decisions, however, did leave them grateful that they did not have to worry too much about several debatable offside calls against them. Also a vicious kick at Henry Newton went unpunished, the midfielder requiring post-match stitches in a shin wound.

Servette: De Blaireville, Schnyder, Morganegg, Martin, Guyot, Sundermann, Pfister, Wegmann, Riner, Andrey, Petrovic. Substitutes: Marchi for Andrey (62), Barriquand for Sundermann (76).

Derby County: Boulton,Webster, Nish, Rioch, Daniel, Todd, Newton, Gemmill, Bourne, Hector, Lee. Substitutes: None used.

Attendance: 9,600
Referee: Mr Woehrer

Post-match positions: n/a

The Rams' success was the only bright spot on an otherwise bleak night for English clubs in the UEFA Cup. Wolverhampton Wanderers defeated FC Porto 3–1 at Molineux, but their earlier poor showing in Portugal saw them eliminated 5–4 on aggregate. Stoke City bravely held Ajax to a scoreless draw in Amsterdam, but with the first leg in the Potteries having ended 1–1 they were also eliminated, away goals counting double in aggregate drawn games. Ipswich Town also perished, as another draw with Twente Enschede, this time 1–1, saw them excluded from the next stage on the away goals calculation. Leeds United, meanwhile, despite losing 2–1 to FC Zurich away from home, progressed to the second round of the European Cup on a 5–3 aggregate. Twenty-four hours earlier, Liverpool had eased into the next stage of the Cup-Winners' Cup – adding another goal to the 11 they had accumulated against Strömsgodset at Anfield, the Merseysiders going through on a 12–0 aggregate.

Other British teams fared little better. Celtic went out of the European Cup 3–1 on aggregate to Greek side Olympiakos, while Cardiff City slumped out of the Cup-Winners' Cup 6–1 overall to Ferencvaros of Hungary. Of the other Scottish sides in action, Dundee were eliminated from the UEFA Cup, although Hibernian progressed at the expense of Rosenborg of Norway. The other Tayside club, Dundee United, fared better than their across-town rivals – eliminating Romanian side Jiul Petroseni on a 3–2 aggregate in the Cup-Winners' Cup.

The carnage among First Division managers continued on 3 October when Dave Sexton was dismissed as the manager of Chelsea. He had been in charge at Stamford Bridge since 1967, and was a well-respected authority on the game. However, after his side had failed to win any of their opening five home matches, most recently losing 1–0 to Wolves, Sexton found that his reputation, and Cup triumphs of the early seventies, counted for little. In reality, he had been under pressure from the opening day of the new campaign, when the club unveiled a state-of-the-art stand costing in excess of £2 million. The

Chelsea chairman Brian Mears had immediately warned Sexton, and the press, that future attendances needed to be above 30,000 to pay for the new structure. Six weeks on, that defeat against the Wanderers had been witnessed by less than two-thirds of the required figure, the home team additionally being jeered off at the end. Sexton's demise, given the earlier events across the capital, meant that of the five senior London sides, only Bertie Mee at Arsenal had remained in office from the start of the season... and that with a mere 10 games of the 42-game schedule completed.

5 October 1974
Football League Division One
West Ham United 2 v Derby County 2

Rams and Hammers provide a feast...

The gloom surrounding football in London was temporarily lifted when these two sides conjured up as good a game as the First Division could produce. Although the 'Blowing Bubbles' chorus was echoing loudly around Upton Park when the Hammers led 2–1, the Rams stuck determinedly to their task and equalised through Kevin Hector. Given their overall contribution to the match, a share of the points was nothing less than they deserved.

West Ham took the early initiative, but their opening goal after nine minutes was as controversial as it was simple. Mervyn Day punted the ball downfield and, once it reached Keith Robson, it was despatched past Colin Boulton with a strike of the highest quality. Despite the Rams defence, to a man, appealing that the Hammers man had controlled the ball with his hand, their protests were to no avail as Mr Walters immediately pointed back to the centre-circle. With Archie Gemmill behind almost everything of worth that the Rams did, the equaliser came on the half-hour. The midfielder fired across a centre and Francis Lee bundled the ball home – it was the striker's fourth goal in six League games, and in all his eighth of the campaign.

Gemmill's efforts were, however, matched by Trevor Brooking's contribution for West Ham, to the extent that either side of the interval the home side looked the better team. Indeed, after 59 minutes Billy Bonds restored their advantage when he rifled a high shot past Boulton, after good approach work from Brooking and Frank Lampard. Given that the visitors had been on European duty in midweek, the fact that they responded so well in the final stages was a credit to them. With 11 minutes remaining, parity was restored when Hector curled a shot past Day from a narrow angle on the right – his equaliser coming after a beautiful build-up involving Colin Todd, Ron Webster and the constantly dangerous Lee. Only Roger Davies was a disappointment in the Rams line up, the irony being that he had been spared the extra midweek fixture because of suspension.

That this was a tremendous encounter was universally recognised in the press box. Norman Fox in *The Times* described it as 'a game that flared and glittered like a Roman candle' – an apt analogy for an enthralling 90 minutes.

West Ham United: Day, McDowell, Lampard, Bonds, Taylor, Lock, Jennings, Paddon, Gould, Brooking, Robson. Substitute: Holland for McDowell (59).

Derby County: Boulton, Webster, Nish, Rioch, Daniel, Newton, Gemmill, Davies, Hector, Lee. Substitute: Bourne.

Attendance: 32,938
Referee: Mr Walters
Post-match positions: Derby 9, West Ham 12

With Lee again on the scoresheet, the former Manchester City striker was already looking to be a superb investment. On the eve of the game in Geneva, he had given reporters a fascinating insight into his thoughts on joining the Rams. 'I don't need to be in soccer for cash these days, but its a long time since I have been happier.' His mood gave as much credit to Dave Mackay as it did to his teammates. The Rams manager had accommodated Lee's personal circumstances without hesitation. Just as had been the case when Mackay arrived at the Baseball Ground as a player, Lee had significant business interests to take care of, and was readily allowed to remain at his north-west base for an extra couple of days each week. As Roy McFarland explained, it certainly did not affect his contribution to the Rams:

'Franny was a magnificent signing for Dave. Franny was proven. I'd played with him for England, and played against him many times. When he came to our place with Manchester City our supporters hated him, but when he settled into our team everybody realised the qualities he had. It was a funny situation at Manchester City because Franny had started to go into business, and was dealing with that side of his life. Everybody in football realised though that he wasn't finished with the game – provided he put his mind to it, and his heart into it. Dave allowed him to do it, and was very good at that type of management. He was very flexible and although Brian was dogmatic, David was a lot easier. He allowed the players more freedom which for us was a bit strange, maybe even initially hard to deal with. Dave just eased and stretched the rules a little bit and allowed us to express ourselves. He did that very well with Franny, it allowed him to do his work with his business and also his football. As everyone knows, it didn't affect his football at Derby County. Franny loved football, when he goes on the football field if he's in your team, he's with you and gives you everything. He gave Derby County two fantastic years, absolutely fantastic, top drawer, top quality.'

The most eagerly awaited result from the games on 5 October was that at Elland Road, where Leeds overcame Arsenal by a 2–0 scoreline. The Yorkshire club had appointed Jimmy

Armfield as their new manager 24 hours beforehand, and were desperate to kick-start their League campaign after the fiasco of Brian Clough's short spell in charge. The 39-year-old joined Leeds after a spell in control of Second Division Bolton Wanderers, the Burnden Park club receiving approximately £12,000 compensation for losing their manager. Middlesbrough maintained their impressive start to the season with a 2–1 home victory over Wolves, Jack Charlton's side moving up to fifth place after their third consecutive win.

At the top of the table, Ipswich remained in first place despite going down to a surprise single-goal defeat against Queen's Park Rangers. After two consecutive defeats Liverpool returned to winning ways with a one-goal victory from their visit to Carlisle United. That defeat for Ipswich at Loftus Road was overshadowed by an incident involving the Rangers centre-half Terry Mancini. The veteran defender staged his own protest at the way the club was being managed by dropping his shorts with his back to the directors' box – his bare-faced cheek going unnoticed by the referee, but later attracting a disrepute charge from the Football Association which brought him a four-game suspension and a £150 fine. Mancini's ill discipline was matched in other Football League fixtures by the dismissal of eight players, the worst day's tally of dismissals since the first round of the FA Cup in 1915.

8 October 1974
Football League Cup 2nd Round
Southampton 5 v Derby County 0

Saints alive!... Rams crash out at the Dell...

After comprehensively defeating Portsmouth in the first round of the League Cup, the Rams returned to the south coast to face

Southampton – another struggling Second Division team. This time, however, Dave Mackay's men were themselves outplayed from the outset and crashed out of the competition in what proved to be the major surprise of the round.

It was hard to believe that this was the same Derby side that had shared in an exhibition of football at West Ham just three days earlier. They allowed the Saints the freedom of the Dell and, once behind, never looked to have the desire to recover. The opening goal came as early as the ninth minute. Colin Todd conceded a free-kick, and although David Peach saw his first shot blocked, the Saints full-back reacted quickly and slammed the rebound into the net. With the home side looking to be in a far more robust mood than the Rams, they increased their lead before the interval. The hard-working Bobby Stokes linked well with Paul Bennett and when the ball reached Mike Channon, the England striker finished in style. Roger Davies went close with a header for the Rams, but it was the sum of their first-half resistance.

In a calculated gamble to change the game, the Rams manager sent on Jeff Bourne, as an additional forward, after 62 minutes. It was not, however, a case of 'cometh the hour, cometh the man'. Within five minutes of the substitution it was 3–0. A corner from Peach was never properly cleared and, as the ball bobbled around, Channon swooped again at Boulton's near post. By the 71st minute, disaster became something more akin to a total humiliation. Peach crossed from the left and, unchallenged, Peter Osgood headed with ease beyond the Rams goalkeeper. With eight minutes remaining the rout was completed with another goal from a corner-kick. Peach crossed to perfection and as the defence hesitated, Channon netted his hat-trick goal. Kevin Hector got clear near the end, but shot tamely at the goalkeeper's legs. It was an effort which summed up the visitors' night.

Mackay was stunned by the Rams' performance. 'It was a terrible result for us. I did not believe we could lose 5–0, Southampton approached it like a cup tie, we did not.' The Rams' interest in the

League Cup was over for another season. Given their display in this game, they looked to be a distance away from being a championship-winning side as well.

Southampton: Turner, McCarthy, Peach, Fisher, Bennett, Mills, Stokes, Channon, Osgood, Holmes, Steele. Substitute: Chatterley for Holmes (82).

Derby County: Boulton, Webster, Nish, Rioch, Daniel, Todd, Newton, Gemmill, Davies, Hector, Lee. Substitute: Bourne for Newton (62).

Attendance: 14,911
Referee: Mr Reynolds
Post-match positions: n/a

---

12 October 1974
Football League Division One
Derby County 1 v Leicester City 0

Rioch strike enough for Rams...

Although this was generally a poor-quality contest, at least the Rams emerged with a nerve-steadying victory, something they desperately needed after their abject midweek display at Southampton. It was certainly not, however, a performance that would have overly worried the representatives of Atlético Madrid sat in the stands prior to the Spanish side's visit to the Baseball Ground in the UEFA Cup on 23 October. With David Nish lining up against his former club, Leicester, missing the injured Dennis Rofe, gave a debut to 20-year-old Steve Yates, the youngster being a cousin of the Rams' left-back.

The home side had the best of the early exchanges, but created nothing to really concern Peter Shilton in the visitors' goal. In fact Leicester almost went ahead after a dreadful error by Henry Newton. The Rams midfielder saw a poor pass easily intercepted by Keith Weller, who raced away, only to shoot wide as Colin Boulton came out to meet him. Soon afterwards, Boulton was again called into action, this time to block an effort from Len Glover. Derby at that stage were struggling to inject any real urgency into their approach play. With the crowd beginning to grow restless, the Rams hit back and took the lead in the 39th minute with a marvellous strike from Bruce Rioch. An understandably nervous Yates failed to contact the ball properly under challenge from Roger Davies, and Rioch reacted quickly and slammed a 25-yarder beyond Shilton and into the corner of the net. After his subdued start to the campaign, Rioch's form had improved significantly in recent games, and the goal clearly inspired him. He again went close before half-time, a fierce volley bringing the very best out of Shilton, the Rams ending the first period clearly on top.

Rather than endeavouring to make the game safe, Derby toiled after the break with both Kevin Hector and Francis Lee looking particularly quiet. That said, they could have gained a couple of penalties – Lee was upended in the box and Graham Cross seemed to handle a cross. However, Mr Nippard, not exactly the Rams' best friend as regards penalty kicks, waved away their credible appeals on both occasions. Overall Leicester created little to threaten Colin Todd and Peter Daniel, their tactic of crowding back behind the ball giving the impression that their manager Jimmy Bloomfield would have settled for a 0–0 draw from the outset.

The victory moved the Rams up to fifth place in the table, three points behind the leaders Ipswich Town who failed to break down Leeds United in a stalemate scoreless draw at Portman Road.

Derby County: Boulton, Webster, Nish, Rioch, Daniel, Todd, Newton, Gemmill, Davies, Hector, Lee. Substitute: Hinton.

Leicester City: Shilton, Whitworth, Yates, Sammels, Munro, Cross, Weller, Earle, Worthington, Birchenall, Glover. Substitute: Stringfellow.

Attendance: 24,753
Referee: Mr Nippard

Post-match positions: Derby 5, Leicester 19

Everyone at the Baseball Ground received a boost on 14 October when Roy McFarland made a return to full training. The Rams defender had undergone an initial period of physical recuperation at the Etwall rehabilitation centre, and looked to be in excellent shape. Sadly, he suffered a further setback after just a few weeks, and rather than being back in action by Christmas, there were just four games of the season remaining when he finally returned to the first team.

After the draw for the second round of the UEFA Cup had been made, the Rams' secretary Stuart Webb announced that ticket prices for the game against Atlético Madrid would be increased. It was a repeat of the policy adopted during the 1972–73 European Cup campaign, when prices had risen for each round as the Rams progressed. For the contest against the Spanish side, while standing prices were increased by 10 pence, at the other end of the scale the most expensive seats in the Centre Stand were marked up from £1.50 to £2. The annual accounts for the year to 31 July 1974 demonstrated the financial importance to the club of the European games. In revealing a small loss of approximately £4,000, the figures for television and other broadcasting fell from £50,000 in the year ending July 1973 – the European Cup year – to just £12,000 for the most recent year when the Rams had not played against any overseas opposition.

In the week following the Leicester game the Rams were also informed by the Football Association that, in the wake of their defeat at Birmingham, Des Anderson had been fined £50 for his post-match comments to the referee. In the other major games on 12 October, Liverpool moved on to the same points total as Ipswich, their 2–0 defeat of Middlesbrough being witnessed by a crowd of 52,590 – the biggest gate of the season to date. Chelsea, meanwhile, admitted that they had failed in an attempt to persuade Frank Blunstone to become their new manager, with the reserve-team coach at Manchester United deciding to remain with the Old Trafford club. It allowed Ron Suart, the former

Blackpool and Blackburn Rovers defender, to continue as Chelsea's caretaker manager, although Eddie McCreadie, a veteran of 331 League games for the Stamford Bridge club, did take over in a permanent role before the end of the season.

15 October 1974
Football League Division One
Sheffield United 1 v Derby County 2

Lee hits brace as Rams extend run...

The Rams achieved their first away win of the season in Sheffield, with a brace from Francis Lee ending the Blades' eight-game unbeaten sequence at Bramall Lane. The only downside for Dave Mackay's side was the booking of four players: Peter Daniel for a handball offence, and annoyingly Kevin Hector, Archie Gemmill and David Nish, who were deemed not to be the mandatory 10 yards away from a free-kick.

The home side, fresh from an entertaining 2–2 draw with Everton, opened up strongly and could have gone ahead in the eighth minute. Tony Currie, the architect behind most of their attacks, moved in from the right side and hit a powerful 25-yard shot which Colin Boulton was happy to turn aside for a corner. Just two minutes later, the Rams countered with a magnificent goal. Colin Todd linked with Hector, who in turn set Gemmill free on the right wing. Gemmill's low centre was perfectly timed and Lee dived in bravely to head decisively beyond the reach of James Brown. The Blades hit back immediately, and for a spell Boulton kept his side in the game. He saved well from Tony Field following an underhit Nish back pass, and in the 25th minute did fantastically well to turn a wickedly deflected volley from Mick Speight away for a corner. From the resulting set piece, although Boulton was beaten, Ron Webster was on the line to head away Keith Eddy's shot.

In the second half, although the Rams, thanks to the hard work of Gemmill in particular, had the majority of the play, they allowed United to equalise after 58 minutes. A long ball into the visitors' defence was picked up by Field, who hit an accurate low drive beyond Boulton and into the far corner. With Lee having an inspired game, Derby sneaked the victory in the 83rd minute. A steady build-up involving several players allowed Webster to centre from the right. Kevin Hector headed the ball down and Lee buried the chance from close range. It took him into double figures for the season, an impressive tally from 17 games. The win extended the Rams' unbeaten League run to six games and moved them into the top three for the first time.

Sheffield United: Brown, Faulkner, Hemsley, Eddy, Colquhoun, Franks, Woodward, Speight, Dearden, Currie, Field. Substitute: Bradford for Franks (55).

Derby County: Boulton, Webster, Nish, Rioch, Daniel, Todd, Newton, Gemmill, Davies, Hector, Lee. Substitute: Powell.

Attendance: 21,882

Referee: Mr Perkin

Post-match positions: Derby 3, Sheffield United 9

19 October 1974
Football League Division One
Carlisle United 3 v Derby County 0

Pathetic Rams lost in the Lakes...

The inconsistency of performance that had appeared in the Rams' League Cup defeat at Southampton was again in evidence against Carlisle United. They gifted the home side two goals and their defence, worryingly for Dave Mackay ahead of the Atlético Madrid game, never looked comfortable against an attack which had scored just three times in the previous eight League fixtures.

The Rams opened up brightly enough and created several promising moves. The best chance fell to Kevin Hector who, after pouncing on a loose ball, only succeeded in hitting the sprawling goalkeeper with a poor shot. As the half progressed, Carlisle settled and both Roger Davies and Francis Lee soon became frustrated at the simple but effective tactics employed by Bill Green and Bob Parker in the heart of the Cumbrians' back four. With the first period looking destined to end scoreless, the home side sneaked a 42nd-minute lead. Frank Clarke forced Colin Boulton into a close-range parry, and although Chris Balderstone mishit the follow up, the ball ran to Ray Train, who prodded his shot just inside the post.

Colin Boulton, ever-present in both Derby County's Championship-winning seasons, a unique achievement, had suffered a rare loss of form in the autumn of 1974 and had to plead with Dave Mackay to keep his place. Against Atlético Madrid he repaid the boss with a penalty save to take the Rams through to the next round of the UEFA Cup.

Whatever Mackay said to his players during the interval seemed to produce the desired effect. Archie Gemmill began prompting those around him, and for a spell the Rams began to improve. However, in the 65th minute they conceded a truly dreadful second goal. David Nish hit a sloppy pass out of defence which allowed Balderstone to deliver a cross into the penalty area. Boulton made a complete hash of getting to the ball and, after Clarke had driven a shot against the upright, Dennis Martin slotted the rebound into the net. Only five more minutes had elapsed before it was 3–0, the beleaguered Rams goalkeeper again being at fault. This time, although he collected a left-wing centre, he then fell over Peter Daniel – the ball spiralling free to Clarke who duly tapped it into the unguarded net.

The final outcome could have been several more. Boulton in particular redeemed himself with a couple of smart saves, and Bob Owen had a goal disallowed for offside. In all it was certainly the Rams' worst display in the League… and that with their UEFA Cup game just four days away.

Carlisle United: Clarke, Carr, Gorman, Balderstone, Green, Parker, Martin, Train, Clarke, Owen, Barry. Substitute: Spearitt.

Derby County: Boulton, Webster, Nish, Rioch, Daniel, Todd, Newton, Gemmill, Davies, Hector, Lee. Substitute: Thomas.

Attendance: 13,353
Referee: Mr Mathewson

Post-match positions: Derby 7, Carlisle United 14

---

23 October 1974
UEFA Cup 2nd Round – 1st Leg
Derby County 2 v Atlético Madrid 2

Madrid goals might prove costly for battling Rams...

Derby County gave themselves a major problem ahead of the second leg of this tie. After conceding two goals to the talented Spanish side, they were in the position of needing to either win or draw at least 3–3 in the Estadio Vincente Calderon on 6 November. The visitors, a skillful and organised unit, remained strong favourites to progress further in the competition after the first leg.

With away goals so often being crucial, Atlético grabbed the lead with a wonderful strike in the 13th minute. A long clearance from the goalkeeper was headed out by Ron Webster, the ball falling to Ayala who took one touch before launching a dipping 30-yard volley past Colin Boulton. Although the goal silenced the home crowd of over 29,000, within two minutes they were celebrating the Rams' equaliser. Reina came out to meet a corner-kick from Archie Gemmill, but only succeeded in punching the ball into the air. Kevin Hector headed it down, and the goalkeeper completed his embarrassment by allowing a mishit David Nish volley to go over him and into the net.

For the remainder of the half, the Rams found themselves largely restricted to hoisting long passes in the direction of the visitors' penalty area.

It was a tactic which produced little, and on the breakaway Madrid often flowed forward with speed and intention. From one such foray, Boulton was forced to dive full-length to his right to deny the impressive Ayala. The Argentinian World Cup player was at the heart of everything Atlético produced, and looked dangerous every time he received the ball. In the 78th minute, Mr Helles, who up till that point had controlled proceedings superbly, gave a controversial penalty decision. Garate chased a pass into the penalty area, stumbled over Webster, and lost control as Boulton dived at his feet. The referee pointed to the spot and, prior to the kick being taken, Aragon, a dead ball specialist, came on as a substitute – his first touch being to slot the ball past Boulton. The Rams, however, refused to give up, and with two minutes remaining they were also awarded a dubious penalty. Francis Lee received the ball with his back to the goal, and under no harsh challenge hit the ground in spectacular style. Bruce Rioch, probably the best player in a Derby shirt, converted the kick to make it 2–2. The action was far from over, however. In the closing seconds Alan Hinton, on for Jeff

Bourne, cut inside from the left wing past defenders and hit the post with a magnificent effort.

Derby County: Boulton, Webster, Nish, Rioch, Daniel, Todd, Newton, Gemmill, Bourne, Hector, Lee. Substitutes: Hinton for Bourne (65).

Atlético Madrid: Reina, Capon, Diaz, Marcellno, Benegas, Eusebio, Leal, Adelardo, Garate, Irureta, Ayala. Substitute: Bermejo for Marcellno (65), Aragon for Leal (78).

Attendance: 29,347
Referee: Mr Helles (France)
Post-match positions: n/a

On the morning after the game, although Mackay admitted that the Spanish side had impressed him, he immediately talked up the Rams' chances of reaching the next stage of the competition. 'I think we have an excellent chance of winning in Madrid. After all, we had the bulk of the play on Wednesday, but I must admit Atlético played better than I anticipated.'

His enthusiasm was not dampened by the announcement of Colin Todd's hospitalisation. The Rams defender had a small lump removed from his groin under local anaesthetic, the prognosis being that he would be absent for three or four matches. He was also withdrawn from the England squad to face Czechoslovakia at Wembley on 30 October in a qualifying game for the 1976 European Championships. With McFarland also injured and David Nish out of favour, it meant that the only Derby player selected within the new England management structure was Steve Powell. The 19-year-old was named as a substitute, also against the Czechs, at Under-23 level at Selhurst Park on the evening before the full international.

With the Rams being the only English side left in the UEFA Cup, their result gained plenty of coverage in the press alongside the performances of Leeds United in European Cup and Liverpool in the Cup-Winners' Cup. The Yorkshire club beat Újpest Dózsa 2–1 away from home, despite having Duncan McKenzie dismissed in the 16th minute. At Anfield, Liverpool conceded a last-minute equaliser to draw 1–1 with Ferencvaros, a scoreline which made the visitors favourites to reach the third round of the competition.

Dave Sexton, who had been axed by Chelsea at the beginning of the month, did not stay out of work for very long. Within two weeks of leaving Stamford Bridge he was unveiled as the new manager of Queen's Park Rangers. Gordon Jago, the man he replaced at Loftus Road, was also quickly back in work, the 42-year-old being appointed to take over at Millwall in place of Benny Fenton.

26 October 1974
Football League Division One
Derby County 2 v Middlesbrough 3

Derby hand visitors easy victory...

This result completed a wretched seven days for the Rams. After being thrashed by Carlisle and generally outplayed by Atlético Madrid, they fell apart against a well-organised Middlesbrough side within which Graeme Souness and John Craggs were outstanding. With Dave Mackay at home nursing a minor head wound following a car accident, Des Anderson took charge of the home side – Steve Powell coming in for Colin Todd and Roger Davies returning, ahead of Jeff Bourne, following his suspension from the UEFA Cup game.

Colin Boulton, who had handed two goals to Carlisle, was again left with a red face after the visitors' opener. In the 11th minute, he allowed a right-side cross from Craggs to slip from his grasp and John Hickton nodded the loose ball unchallenged into the net. To their credit, after falling behind to yet another early goal, the Rams hit back purposefully. David Nish put a good effort just wide and a 35th-minute shot from Kevin Hector hit left-back Frank Spraggon on the line. If that had gone in and levelled the contest, the outcome might have been different. Instead, within a minute, Jack Charlton's side had doubled their advantage. A cross to the far post was headed back across the goal by Hickton, and Alan Foggon completed the move in style from close range. Almost immediately from the restart, Hector finally got the home side on the scoreboard. Francis Lee dribbled his way to the narrowest of angles, but still managed to steer a pass to Hector, who scored with the simplest of finishes.

With the Baseball Ground faithful anticipating a second-half revival, the visitors went further ahead within three minutes. It was certainly the best goal of the game: Foggon sent David Mills clear on the right and, as Boulton advanced towards him, the pacey striker chipped the ball perfectly into the far corner of the net. Rather than increasing their urgency and putting pressure on the visitors' defence, Derby fumbled around for the rest of the game and, at times, looked completely devoid of inspiration. As a consequence, the Middlesbrough goalkeeper Jim Platt found himself largely relegated to the role of a spectator. The 68th-minute introduction of Alan Hinton, surprisingly in place of Bruce Rioch, who had done more than most, did not unduly change the pattern of play. It was Hinton, however, who recorded the Rams' second goal – albeit a mere injury-time consolation. The left-winger drove home a loose ball which gave the scoreline an artificial air of respectability. The victory lifted the visitors into the top four and contributed to Jack Charlton later being named as the manager of the month.

As the Rams trudged off, with Roy McFarland and Colin Todd in the stands, their reputation as a classy organised outfit seemed to be in tatters.

Derby County: Boulton, Webster, Nish, Rioch, Daniel, Powell, Newton, Gemmill, Davies, Hector, Lee. Substitute: Hinton for Rioch (68).

Middlesbrough: Platt, Craggs, Spraggon, Souness, Boam, Maddren, Murdoch, Mills, Hickton, Foggon, Armstrong. Substitute: Willey.

Attendance: 24,036
Referee: Mr Wallace

Post-match positions: Derby 7, Middlesbrough 4

Division One – 26 October 1974

		P	W	D	L	GF	GA	PTS
1	Liverpool	14	10	1	3	22	8	21
2	Manchester City	15	8	4	3	20	16	20
3	Ipswich Town	15	8	2	5	19	10	18
4	Middlesbrough	14	7	4	3	22	16	18
5	Everton	15	4	10	1	20	17	18
6	Stoke City	14	6	5	3	23	18	17
7	**Derby County**	**15**	**5**	**6**	**4**	**23**	**22**	**16**
8	Burnley	15	7	2	6	24	24	16
9	Sheffield United	15	6	4	5	22	26	16
10	Newcastle United	14	5	5	4	19	20	15
11	West Ham United	15	5	4	6	25	25	14
12	Birmingham City	15	6	2	7	22	23	14
13	Wolverhampton Wdrs	13	4	6	5	16	17	14
14	Coventry City	14	4	6	4	20	24	14
15	Carlisle United	15	5	3	7	13	14	13
16	Leicester City	13	4	4	5	17	18	12
17	Chelsea	14	3	6	5	16	23	12
18	Leeds United	14	4	3	7	16	16	11
19	Queen's Park Rangers	14	3	5	6	13	17	11
20	Tottenham Hotspur	14	4	2	8	17	21	10
21	Arsenal	14	3	3	8	15	20	9
22	Luton Town	15	1	7	7	13	22	9

RON WEBSTER

CHAPTER FOUR
November

Rams sneak rare win at Elland Road...

Derby County's goal at Elland Road was a long time in the making – 619 minutes to be precise. The last Rams player to score at Leeds had been Arthur Stewart – and that was in the 89th minute of the 1967–68 League Cup semi-final. Dave Mackay was forced to make a late adjustment to his line-up: Colin Todd suffered a reaction to his groin operation, so Steve Powell retained his place in the back four. Opposing the Rams in midfield was John O'Hare, who impressed with a forceful display against his former colleagues.

With Leeds attacking from the outset, the visitors employed a defensive policy of leaving Francis Lee as a lone attacker. As a consequence, the home team had much the better of the first-half play. Fortunately for the Rams, Colin Boulton made a welcome return to form, his save midway through the period from a diving O'Hare header being particularly impressive. He also saved well from Terry Yorath and Allan Clarke – the renowned Leeds marksman for once having got the better of his 'shadow' Ron Webster.

After the interval, the play continued in similar vein. However, much as Jimmy Armfield's team attacked with purpose, the Rams defence, with Powell giving a superb performance, held firm. Of the chances United did create, Peter Lorimer hit the bar and Gordon McQueen headed well wide from a good position. The game took a farcical turn moments before Duncan McKenzie's arrival in the 64th minute. The player, much admired by Dave Mackay, was spoken to by a policeman as he warmed up, the ill-informed officer apparently believing that Mackenzie was a spectator about to invade the pitch. The Rams did not pose a real attacking threat until 12 minutes from time. Then David Nish broke away on the left flank and fed his pass inside to Francis Lee. The Rams striker looked up and steadied himself, and then struck a superb effort past David Harvey from 25 yards. It was just one of four shots the visitors mustered in the entire 90 minutes. As is the way in games between these two sides, the referee usually completes the contest with a full notebook. Accordingly, Bruce Rioch and Yorath were cautioned before half-time, with Mr New adding the names of Roger Davies, Powell and Terry Cooper after the interval.

The Rams manager was understandably delighted with the victory and the goal from Lee – 'A magnificent effort, typical of the man.' The nature of the success was also the source of a couple of interesting Monday morning headlines. Denis Lowe's report in the *Daily Telegraph* was titled 'Lee the bandit in Leeds robbery.' Meanwhile, in *The Guardian*, Alan Dunn's piece was headed 'Freak win for Derby.' It mattered little of course to the Rams players, who had travelled home with their minds already set on producing a similar rearguard action in Madrid four days later.

Leeds United: Harvey, Reaney, Cooper, Yorath, McQueen, Hunter, Lorimer, Clarke, O'Hare, Giles, Madeley. Substitute: McKenzie for Lorimer (64).

Derby County: Boulton, Webster, Nish, Rioch, Daniel, Powell, Newton, Gemmill, Davies, Hector, Lee. Substitute: Macken.

Attendance: 33,551

Referee: Mr New

Post-match positions: Derby 7, Leeds 19

**6 November 1974
UEFA Cup 2nd Round – 2nd leg**
Atlético Madrid 2 v Derby County 2
(aggregate 4–4) (Derby won 7–6 on penalties)

Magnificent...simply magnificent!...

Derby County defied the odds on a memorable night at the Vincente Calderon stadium in Madrid. Despite falling behind to an early goal, they battled back to take the lead and, after a pulsating two hours of action, eventually resolved the outcome of the tie in a nail-biting sudden-death penalty competition. Amazingly, the Rams' best result under the management of Dave Mackay was achieved without both Roy McFarland and Colin Todd. To a man, the 11 who represented Derby County in this contest were magnificent. If a man of the match had to be chosen, it would have been Todd's replacement Steve Powell, who gave an assured display which belied his years.

After the 2–2 draw at the Baseball Ground, Mackay's plan was to keep the game level with the hope of sneaking a breakaway goal. It was a strategy which was shattered within the first four minutes. The German referee dubiously awarded Madrid a free-kick, for apparently nothing more than the slightest of nudges on Ayala by Archie Gemmill. The ball was delivered into the penalty area, and 37-year-old Luis headed unchallenged past Colin Boulton. It was the first, and last, moment of total uncertainty in the visitors' defence. The Rams struck back and created two good chances before half-time. Francis Lee was forced wide after bypassing Reina, that opportunity being followed by a Bruce Rioch shot which

Steve Powell and Archie Gemmill watch this attempt at goal by an Atlético Madrid player at the Vicente Calderon Stadium.

went over the top. Although those efforts came to nothing, the sweeping nature of the visitors' counter-attacks was encouraging, their enterprise eventually being rewarded within 10 minutes of the restart.

In the 55th minute, Kevin Hector got clear on the left and his beautiful centre was headed down to Rioch by the imposing Roger Davies. The midfielder did not waste his second chance: his run into the area was timed to perfection, the drive past the goalkeeper unstoppable. Just 10 minutes later the Spanish crowd were stunned into silence when Hector put the Rams in front. A neat move between Gemmill and Lee allowed the inspired Scot, in his 200th senior game for the club, to centre to Hector, who chested down and blasted the ball home. The drama increased further in the 76th minute. Henry Newton was adjudged to have handled the ball and Luis completed his brace with a 25-yard free-kick past Boulton. There was no addition to the scoreline in the remaining 14 minutes, or indeed the 30 minutes of extra time.

The penalty competition simply increased the tension swirling around the stadium. In the first stage of five kicks per team, both sides netted four: Rioch, Hector, Nish and Lee all scoring – Davies having his effort well saved by Reina. The sudden death extension saw Gemmill, Newton and Powell all hit the net, the crucial 16th spot kick from Eusebio being superbly parried onto a post by Boulton.

Atlético Madrid: Reina, Capon, Diaz, Adelardo, Benegas, Eusebio, Alberto, Luis, Garate, Irureta, Ayala. Substitutes: Marcellno for Adelardo (45), Salcedo for Alberto (61).

Derby County: Boulton, Webster, Nish, Rioch, Daniel, Powell, Newton, Gemmill, Davies, Hector, Lee. Substitutes: None used.

Attendance: 35,000

Referee: Mr Biwerst (West Germany)

Post-match positions: n/a

An ecstatic Rams manager summed up the drama of the evening: 'What an incredible game for sheer spectacle. I cannot remember seeing anything quite like it.' It was a night to make any supporter of the club immensely proud. Archie Gemmill's contribution over the two hours was immense. He produced a performance of the highest quality, his best of the season, and quite probably his entire Baseball Ground career. As the teams finally departed, he was hugged warmly by Juan Carlos Lorenzo, the defeated manager, who offered the Rams captain the warmest of congratulations. In the press conference after the game Lorenzo heaped further praise on the visitors, admitting to reporters that he never seen a British side attack so much away from home. It was certainly a major shock to the Spaniards to be beaten. The value they had placed on the contest was reflected in the fact that they were apparently on a incentive of £1,000 per man to progress – a figure which completely dwarfed the Rams' bonus of a mere £30 per player.

Throughout his time with the Rams, and indeed later at Nottingham Forest, Gemmill was praised, largely, merely for his ability to cover ground. It was, and remains, a bone of contention with the man from Paisley:

'People remember me as someone who gave 100 percent

and ran all over the pitch. But if you look through the moves when Derby County scored, I was involved in a reasonable amount of them. Running was obviously an important part of my game, but just last year the gaffer [Brian Clough] was looking at a Derby tape, and he said that he had never realised what a good player I was. The running capacity was something which caught the eye, more so than the fact that I could actually pass and head the ball – sometimes those things get overlooked.'

In the European Cup, Leeds United eased into the third round with a 3–0 victory at Elland Road against Újpest Dózsa, goals from Gordon McQueen, Billy Bremner and Terry Yorath giving the Yorkshire side a 5–1 aggregate victory. In the Cup-Winners' Cup Liverpool drew 0–0 against Ferencvaros but, with the teams having drawn 1–1 earlier at Anfield, they were eliminated on the away goal rule. In the same competition, Dundee United were also eliminated after being defeated by Bursapor of Turkey. With both Dundee and Hibernian also crashing out of the UEFA Cup, Leeds and Derby were left as the only British sides remaining in the European competitions.

---

9 November 1974
Football League Division One
Derby County 5 v Queen's Park Rangers 2

Hector hits three in Rams goal frenzy...

After their marvellous result in Spain, the Rams overwhelmed Queen's Park Rangers with a dazzling demonstration of attacking football. The victory crowned a fantastic eight days for Dave Mackay's team – remarkably coming on the back of the doom and gloom that had engulfed the Baseball Ground after the 3–2 defeat by Middlesbrough on 26 October.

Perhaps not surprisingly, after their midweek exertions, the Rams started slowly and the London side had the best of the midfield exchanges. Within 20 minutes, however, Derby had control and could have opened their account in the 27th minute. Bruce Rioch surged into the penalty area and was felled by Gerry Francis. The referee gave the penalty and Rioch himself took the kick, his powerful drive going beyond the left hand of Phil Parkes and into the net. The linesman, however, indicated that Archie Gemmill had encroached into the area. Rioch retook the kick, but second time around Parkes blocked his shot at the foot of the post.

Kevin Hector hit a hat-trick as Derby thrashed Queen's Park Rangers 5–2 in early November.

The Rams' frustration did not last for long. Just six more minutes had passed before Kevin Hector netted the opener. The Rangers goalkeeper did well to parry a fierce cross shot from Francis Lee, but was left helpless as Hector reacted smartly and slotted in the rebound. After 36 minutes it was 2–0. Rioch set off on a run past three defenders and hammered a drive across Parkes and into the far corner. With the Rams looking good value for a two-goal half-time advantage, they allowed the visitors back into the game with a 44th-minute reply. A long free-kick caused problems in the Derby defence, and although Henry Newton got to the ball, his mistimed clearance fell to Mick Leach, who gratefully accepted the chance.

The Rams looked revitalised after the interval and Hector went on to complete a superb hat-trick, the 11th of his professional career. After 55 minutes, Rioch – who had a fine game – delivered a cross from the left for Hector to chest down and smash past the despairing dive of Parkes. Thirteen minutes later Gemmill, playing with a hamstring injury, dispossessed Dave Thomas out wide before centering for Hector to score from close range. At 4–1 ahead, Mackay opted to withdraw Gemmill in favour of Jeff Bourne, who had missed out in Madrid following the return of Roger Davies from suspension. Obviously keen to impress, Bourne quickly got involved in the contest and set up the fifth goal. He ran at speed towards the by now dishevelled Rangers defence, before slipping the ball to Lee who cracked a drive beyond the reach of Parkes.

The visitors netted the final score in the dying embers of the contest, when their largely anonymous talisman Stanley Bowles opted to make a contribution. He demonstrated his obvious talents with a tantalising run and finish past Colin Boulton – in what was the best goal of the afternoon. The Rams acknowledged their fans from the centre-circle at the end. The day's only disappointment was that only 23,339 had bothered to turn out and witness such an inspired performance.

Derby County: Boulton, Webster, Nish, Rioch, Daniel, Powell, Newton, Gemmill, Davies, Hector, Lee. Substitute: Bourne for Gemmill (69).

Queen's Park Rangers: Parkes, Clement, Gillard, Hazell, Mclintock, Webb, Thomas, Francis, Leach, Bowles, Givens. Substitute: Rogers.

Attendance: 23,339

Referee: Mr Smith

Post-match positions: Derby 5, Queen's Park Rangers 18

Elsewhere in the First Division on 9 November, Manchester City moved to the top of the table with a single-goal success over Stoke City, a contest which marked a 500th club appearance for City's Alan Oakes. Liverpool's poor run of form continued with a 3–1 home defeat against Arsenal, as Gunners captain Alan Ball netted a brace of goals. Although Everton gained a point after a 1–1 draw against Tottenham Hotspur at White Hart Lane, they were again widely criticised in the press for their style of play, the draw being their 11th in 17 fixtures.

In the midweek matches, there was a major shock in the fourth round of the League Cup. Fourth Division Chester humbled Leeds 3–0 in North Wales, John James netting two goals for the hosts, who completely outplayed their visitors. Elsewhere in the competition, Manchester United beat Burnley 3–2 at Old Trafford, while Middlesbrough sneaked a one-goal victory at Anfield, that result coming as Liverpool attempted to resolve their midfield worries by signing Terry McDermott from Newcastle United for a fee of £170,000. Also on Merseyside, Third Division Tranmere Rovers announced that Bill Shankly had agreed to help them by taking on an advisory role alongside their manager Ron Yeats – who had of course been one of Shankly's prodigies at Liverpool in the early sixties.

The Rams' preparations for their trip to Arsenal received a boost with the news that Colin Todd had regained full fitness after his groin operation. With Gemmill also responding to treatment on his hamstring strain, it gave Mackay, with the exception of Roy McFarland, a full squad to choose from as the Rams went into the match with a poor away record against the Londoners. With the exception of a 1–0 win in 1972–73, Arsenal had won the other four League games since the Rams' return to the First Division – most noticeably by a 4–0 margin on 8 November 1969.

16 November 1974
Football League Division One
Arsenal 3 v Derby County 1

Todd returns, but Gunners shoot down Rams...

The Rams slipped to another defeat at Highbury against an Arsenal side that had taken five points from the previous six. Colin Todd returned for the visitors in his 150th appearance for the club, Steve Powell, his replacement for four games, preferring a 90-minute run out with the second team rather than taking a seat on the substitutes' bench. Arsenal included Terry Mancini in their line up, the bald-headed defender having moved across London from Queen's Park Rangers in a £20,000 deal.

Surprisingly for two sides on the top of their form, the first half produced little incident of real note. The Gunners employed a long ball game with the intention of freeing up their twin strike force of John Radford and Brian Kidd. With the Rams midfield duly starved of possession, their attack was stagnant for long periods with only Francis Lee looking capable of posing the Arsenal back four any serious problems. Of the few chances in the opening stanza, Radford forced Colin Boulton into a diving save, while at the other end Bruce Rioch had a shot hacked off the line by Bob McNab.

The match desperately need a goal to lift it from its mediocrity, and Arsenal duly obliged in the 52nd minute. Radford slipped a pass to Alan Ball, and the former England midfielder curled a shot past Boulton from the edge of the penalty area – the goalkeeper's chances of making the save evaporating when the ball bounced awkwardly in front of him as he dived. In the 72nd minute Ball was the instigator of the second Arsenal goal. He got clear on the right-hand side and, as Derby appealed for offside, his low cross was swept home by Kidd, the former Manchester United man having rediscovered his scoring touch since a £100,000 move from Old Trafford.

With just 18 minutes remaining, Dave Mackay's side looked to be well and truly beaten. Lee gave them a glimmer of hope, however, when he won a 75th minute penalty following a tackle by Peter Simpson. Rioch, the Rams' best midfielder, slammed in the spot-kick, the power of his strike being such that Jimmy Rimmer was motionless as the ball whizzed past him. Having awarded one slightly suspicious penalty, Mr Rice opted to even things up moments later. As Arsenal pressed forward, Peter Daniel seemed to have won the ball fairly in a challenge with Kidd, but another spot-kick was awarded. Ball, the Gunners' skipper, took the penalty and sent Boulton the wrong way to seal the victory.

Arsenal: Rimmer, Rice, McNab, Kelly, Mancini, Simpson, Storey, Ball, Radford, Kidd, Brady. Substitute: George.

Derby County: Boulton, Webster, Nish, Rioch, Daniel, Todd, Newton, Gemmill, Davies, Hector, Lee. Substitute: Bourne.

Attendance: 32,286
Referee: Mr Rice
Post-match positions: Derby 10, Arsenal 18

Birmingham City grabbed the surprise headlines after the weekend, with two goals from Kenny Burns helping them to an impressive 4–0 win at home against Manchester City. In the lower divisions, Notts County's Ian Scanlon netted a hat-trick in under three minutes as his side defeated Sheffield Wednesday – a feat the teams in Northern Spain could only dream about, as referees in Catalonia staged a day's strike in protest at the language used against them by supporters.

With Todd coming through his return game unscathed, he was able to join up with the rest of the England squad for their European Championship qualification game against Portugal at Wembley on 20 November. Don Revie's side could not, however, produce a repeat of their performance against Czechoslovakia three weeks earlier, and were held to a disappointing scoreless draw. Todd was named among the substitutes for the game, but was called into action after just 25 minutes, the Rams defender replacing the Leeds United full-back Terry Cooper who limped off after a heavy challenge. In other qualification games, although Scotland were beaten 2–1 by Spain, Wales – who included Rod Thomas in their side – thrashed Luxembourg 5–0 in Swansea.

Two days later Peter Shilton, who had been in goal for England at Wembley, finally completed his long-sought move away from Leicester City. He signed for Stoke City in a deal which netted his former club a fee of £335,000 – a new British record for a goalkeeper. It was a transfer which again confirmed the ambition of the Potteries club, the transaction for Shilton taking their expenditure over the previous nine months to in excess of £750,000 after the arrivals of Alan Hudson from Chelsea and Geoff Salmons from Sheffield United. Another goalkeeper in the news was Bill Glazier, who, after an early season injury, was named in the Coventry City team to face Arsenal on 23 November. The game marked his 400th appearance for the Sky Blues, a fixture they subsequently won 3–0.

With Leicester struggling at the wrong end of the table, they were obviously keen to strengthen their squad with the money received from the sale of Shilton. They agreed a fee of £150,000 with Liverpool for John Toshack, but after announcing the transfer, pulled out when their medical staff baulked at the extent of Toshack's injury problems. The Welsh striker had missed a number of games over the previous year due to a calcification of his left thigh.

23 November 1974
Football League Division One
Derby County 2 v Ipswich Town 0

Rams defeat leaders in Baseball Ground mudbath...

The final score at the Baseball Ground did not reflect the Rams' domination of this contest. Indeed, had it not been for Laurie Sivell in the Ipswich goal, Derby would most likely have netted five at home for the second successive game. Colin Boulton, meanwhile, had just one save to make as the players in front of him extinguished any threat that the visitors created. The Ipswich manager Bobby Robson was not helped by his pre-match selection worries: his defence was short of Kevin Beattie with a viral infection, and Alan Hunter who was suspended.

The Rams beat League leaders Ipswich Town 2–0 in late November. Kevin Hector heads home for Derby past keeper Laurie Sivell. Francis Lee and Roger Davies are the other Rams players in view, while future Derby manager George Burley wears the number two shirt for Ipswich (far right).

The Rams made a perfect start and were ahead by the eighth minute. Bruce Rioch, who at times created havoc with his intelligent running, won a corner on the right. He took the kick himself and, in a rehearsed move, rolled the ball for Henry Newton who, in turn, chipped perfectly for Kevin Hector to head beyond Sivell and into the net. As the Rams continued to press forward, it was not just Rioch who looked to be in irresistible form. Newton, often the man behind much of the 'unnoticed' yet vital work in the centre of the pitch, also had a marvellous game. In the 28th minute, it was

Newton who set up the Rams' second goal. After receiving a pass from Francis Lee, he switched play to the left with a neat square pass into Rioch's path. On his favoured left foot at the edge of the penalty area, Rioch could be deadly – and on this occasion the ball arrowed into the net off the far post.

After the interval, the home side created chance after chance. Sivell frustrated Lee with two smart stops, and Hector also had efforts blocked by an Ipswich rearguard which at times looked totally bewildered – such was the speed and precision of the Rams' thrusts into their penalty area. The pitch, which in places resembled a mudbath, only served to make the display even more impressive. Alongside Rioch and Newton, Archie Gemmill thrived in the conditions, his workrate and accuracy of pass remarkable given the fact that he was playing despite not being 100 percent fit.

With Colin Todd and Peter Daniel at times looking immaculate, the pre-game table toppers were restricted to a first-half shot from Colin Harper which Boulton saved with his legs. To a man, Dave Mackay's team out ran and out thought their opponents and fully deserved the points – vital ones given the congested nature of the First Division table. With Manchester City beating Leicester City 4–1 at Maine Road to claim top position, the Rams jumped five places up to fifth, just a couple of points behind the Mancunian club, although only three points covered the top eight teams.

Derby County: Boulton, Webster, Nish, Rioch, Daniel, Todd, Newton, Gemmill, Davies, Hector, Lee. Substitute: Bourne.

Ipswich Town: Sivell, Burley, Harper, Talbot, Peddelty, Mills, Hamilton, Viljoen, Johnson, Whymark, Woods. Substitute: Osborne for Viljoen (64).

Attendance: 24,341

Referee: Mr Homewood

Post-match positions: Derby 5, Ipswich Town 3

27 November 1974
UEFA Cup 3rd Round – 1st Leg
Derby County 3 v Velez Mostar 1

Substitutes make the difference against Yugoslavians...

Although the Rams built up a two-goal lead ahead of the second leg on 11 December, they trailed the visitors until the last 20 minutes and only came to life after the introduction of Jeff Bourne and Alan Hinton. On a pitch that had deteriorated following the Ipswich game, good football was at a premium, yet the Yugoslavians – on their first visit to England – impressed observers with the flair of their attacking play, particularly in the first half.

Just as had been the case in Madrid, the Rams fell behind to an early goal. Only two minutes had elapsed when Hadziabdic hit a 40-yard pass out to Topic on the right wing. Although Colin Todd attempted to clear the low cross, the ball stuck in the mud and fell to Vladic, who smashed it past Colin Boulton. With Bruce Rioch making intelligent use of the firmer surface out on the flanks, Derby responded well and could have equalised when a lunging Francis Lee just failed to make contact with a Kevin Hector pass across the front of goal. Lee also went close when a David Nish corner was headed down to him by Roger Davies – unfortunately the burly striker's shot went over the top from close range. The Rams improved as the contest progressed, but still looked vulnerable when the visitors attacked on the breakaway. Vukoje got clear and was fouled by Peter Daniel, the free-kick from Vladic being tipped over by Boulton.

With an hour played, Dave Mackay decided to make a change and Bourne came on in place of Davies, who had struggled in the conditions. Bourne responded well to the call and the Rams' attacks started to look far more dangerous. The introduction of Alan Hinton in the 69th minute eventually produced the equaliser. The speedy left-winger gave Velez something different to contend with and three minutes later the crowd of 26,131 erupted. Hector delivered the ball in from the right and Bourne was on hand to guide a shot past the goalkeeper. With 12 minutes remaining, Hinton turned back the clock with a trademark piledriver of a shot. After receiving the ball with his back to goal, the popular veteran hit a superb effort on the turn into the far corner of the net.

In the closing minutes the visitors fell into a state of panic. In the 89th minute Bourne netted his second from close range after Archie Gemmill had worked wonders out on the right wing. The pressure proved too much for Gladovic, the Goliath-like Velez centre-half. He headbutted Bourne and was dismissed by the East German referee. A worrying sight for Mackay, however, was Nish sliding in the mud and into the terrace wall. He appeared to have suffered injuries to both his ankle and hand, to add to the Rams' growing list of problems: Lee, Gemmill and Hector had all played despite carrying an assortment of injuries.

Derby County: Boulton, Webster, Nish, Rioch, Daniel, Todd, Newton, Gemmill, Davies, Hector, Lee. Substitutes: Bourne for Davies (59), Hinton for Lee (69).

Velez Mostar: Mrgan, Colic, Hadziabdic, Primorac, Gladovic, Pecejl, Topic, Vladic, Vukoje, Ledic, Hodzic. Substitute: Okuka for Vladic (61).

Attendance: 26,131
Referee: Mr Mannig (East Germany)
Post-match positions: n/a

The attendance of 26,131 was below Mackay's pre-match expectation of a gate in excess of 30,000. Speaking to Jeff Falmer of the *Daily Mail* ahead of the game, the Rams boss had given his thoughts on the crowds at the Baseball Ground, which were down by 15 percent on average on the previous year. In estimating that between 2,000–3,000 fans were staying away because Brian Clough had left, he said 'After the way we have been playing this season, I think many of them want to come back – but they have said that they would never come back, and are frightened that friends and neighbours might have a go at them.' With the pro-Clough movement boasting a membership of more than 10,000, there was obviously a lot of truth in Mackay's statement. However, other factors were undoubtably influencing the turnout: hooliganism, worries about unemployment and, to a lesser extent, the extended IRA bombing campaign on the mainland. All of these were having an effect on football attendances generally.

Away from the European games, there were several other significant fixtures. A goal from Mike Channon gave Southampton a 1–0 victory over Newcastle United in the first leg of the Texaco Cup final – the competition that the Rams had won, in addition to the Championship, in the 1971–72 campaign. In the First Division, Stoke City also enjoyed a single-goal victory, a ninth-minute strike from Geoff Hurst giving them the points at home to Queen's Park Rangers. At White Hart Lane, a testimonial crowd of over 22,000 raised in excess of £10,000 for Alan Gilzean – Tottenham Hotspur

Jeff Bourne scored in the 2–2 draw with Liverpool at Anfield in December. On the previous Wednesday he had scored two after coming on as substitute against Velez Mostar in the UEFA Cup third round first leg. Signed from local Linton United in 1969, Bourne hadn't figured much under Clough but Dave Mackay liked him and gave him a run as a regular in the second half of 1973–74. The arrival of Francis Lee in the summer meant Bourne was more of a cover striker, but he featured in 27 League and Cup games in the Championship season, 14 of them starts.

beating Red Star Belgrade 2–0. Meanwhile, in Tony Book's benefit game at Maine Road, an All Star team which included George Best, Kevin Keegan and Bobby Charlton beat Manchester City 6–4 – the Mancunian crowd of around 15,000 adding a further £8,000 to Book's testimonial fund.

The Rams' game at home to Wolverhampton Wanderers on 30 November was postponed after the Baseball Ground surface finally sucumbed to the rains of autumn. With ankle-deep mud covering large areas of the pitch, the match referee Mr Challis had no hesitation in calling off the contest at 10am – thankfully early enough to prevent the supporters of both teams from commencing their journeys to the game. Although the postponement gave the Rams an extra fixture to fit in, at least the players who were carrying injuries had the chance to gain an extra period of rest and treatment.

In an otherwise full schedule of First Division fixtures Manchester City and Burnley each netted a quartet of goals. Barney Daniels scored twice in his first game of the season for City as they beat Leicester 4–1 at Maine Road. At Turf Moor, meanwhile, although Peter Noble scored a hat-trick as Burnley also won 4–1 against Newcastle, the result was overshadowed by the fact that United's John Tudor required seven stitches in a head wound after a brick was thrown through the window of the team coach as it left the ground.

Division One – 30 November 1974

		P	W	D	L	GF	GA	PTS
1	Stoke City	20	9	7	4	33	25	25
2	Ipswich Town	20	11	2	7	28	15	24
3	Liverpool	19	10	4	5	25	14	24
4	Everton	19	6	12	1	27	19	24
5	Manchester City	20	10	4	6	26	25	24
6	West Ham United	20	9	5	6	37	28	23
7	**Derby County**	**19**	**8**	**6**	**5**	**32**	**27**	**22**
8	Newcastle United	19	8	6	5	28	25	22
9	Burnley	20	9	4	7	35	32	22
10	Sheffield United	19	8	5	6	27	30	21
11	Birmingham City	20	8	4	8	31	29	20
12	Middlesbrough	19	7	6	6	25	26	20
13	Leeds United	19	7	4	8	25	21	18
14	Wolverhampton Wdrs	19	5	8	6	22	25	18
15	Coventry City	20	5	8	7	28	37	18
16	Tottenham Hotspur	19	6	5	8	23	25	17
17	Queen's Park Rangers	20	6	5	9	23	27	17
18	Arsenal	19	6	4	9	23	25	16
19	Leicester City	18	5	5	8	20	25	15
20	Chelsea	19	3	8	8	19	35	14
21	Carlisle United	20	5	3	12	17	24	13
22	Luton Town	19	1	7	11	17	31	9

CHAPTER FIVE

December

As the Rams prepared for their visit to Anfield on 7 December, Dave Mackay finally dismissed newspaper reports that were, once again, linking him to Stan Bowles. 'On the evidence of his display here at the Baseball Ground, I have not got the slightest interest in him' he told reporters, 'Over the longer term Jeff Bourne will be a better player for us.' In naming his side for the trip to Merseyside, Mackay opted to keep the same team that would have played against Wolverhampton Wanderers, with Bourne, after his 'super sub' display from the bench against Velez, retaining his place ahead of Roger Davies. With David Nish having undergone minor surgery on his hand, the 'forgotten man' Rod Thomas was also included for just his second League appearance of the campaign. The manager also took time to praise Peter Daniel, who was benefiting from an extended run in the first team. 'Peter has been outstanding, and has done better than I anticipated.' The quiet no-nonsense defender had certainly not let anybody down during the first three months of the campaign, and looked to be a better quality player than the £70,000 Luton Town had offered for him towards the end of their Second Division promotion campaign.

Ahead of the weekend's games, Arsenal signed 23-year-old Alex

Cropley from Hibernian for a fee of £150,000, the Highbury club having been keen to add the midfielder to their squad for several months. Elsewhere in London, Queen's Park Rangers opened negotiations with Notts County for Don Masson, the midfielder subsequently moving to Loftus Road in a £100,000 transfer on 10 December.

7 December 1974
Football League Division One
Liverpool 2 v Derby County 2

Davies on scoresheet, Rams gain vital point...

The Rams came away from Merseyside satisfied with a hard-earned point. A late strike from substitute Roger Davies gave them a 2–2 draw in a contest that was played, almost throughout, at a frantic pace. Dave Mackay's pre-match plan to go to Anfield and attack was characteristically bold, but his decision was rewarded with an early goal.

In the 13th minute, Henry Newton – who had another excellent game – sent Bruce Rioch away on the right with a well-timed pass. After beating both Alec Lindsay and Peter Cormack with ease, the robust midfielder's low centre was turned in by Jeff Bourne. Within moments it could have been 2–0. Bourne went past Tommy Smith, but his cross, delivered from the right, just eluded Kevin Hector at the far post. That half chance only served to stir Liverpool into making a stinging response – and indeed within four minutes they had levelled the game, and then gone ahead. After 18 minutes, the veteran Ian Callaghan cleverly worked himself an opportunity and, although his curling shot came back off the bar, Ray Kennedy reacted quickly and tapped in the rebound from close range. Then, in the 22nd minute, the Reds won a corner and Smith drove in a shot which the alert Steve Heighway diverted into the corner of the net with his head.

COLIN TODD

To their credit, Derby refused to accept that defeat at 'Fortress Anfield' was a probability. Their optimism was based on the fact that Liverpool had failed to win any of their previous three home games – an unthinkable prospect in the heyday of Bill Shankly. The legendary Scot watched the contest from the directors' box, and no doubt returned home worried by the lack of efficiency displayed by several of the Reds players. As the Rams hit back, Rioch had a chance to restore parity before the interval. His shot from a free-kick hit the outside of a post, but with the defensive wall just five yards away, Mr Willis ordered the set piece to be retaken and the danger was cleared.

In the second half, although the visitors had the better of the play, they had nothing to show until Davies replaced Hector with 20 minutes remaining. Davies, who had lost his place in the line-up to Bourne, set out with a purpose. He immediately began to create problems for the Liverpool defence, and was rewarded in the 83rd minute. Colin Todd received a pass from the energetic Archie Gemmill, his chipped centre being headed past Ray Clemence by Davies for the striker's first goal since 14 September at Birmingham.

In the Rams defence, Rod Thomas showed no signs of a lack of match practice, and Ron Webster again remained calm whenever Liverpool increased the pressure on him via their left flank.

Liverpool: Clemence, Smith, Lindsay, Thompson, Cormack, Hughes, Keegan, McDermott, Heighway, Kennedy, Callaghan. Substitute: Hall.

Derby County: Boulton, Webster, Thomas, Rioch, Daniel, Todd, Newton, Gemmill, Bourne, Hector, Lee. Substitute: Davies for Hector (70).

Attendance: 41,058
Referee: Mr Willis

Post-match positions: Derby 8, Liverpool 4

The Rams' performance against Liverpool was typical of Mackay's adventurous approach to the game. Roy McFarland is a firm believer that he brought the same theory to management as he had done to playing:

'Dave's theory was he wanted to win. He was the best winner I ever played with – and was privileged to play with and train with and be part of. The education I learned from him as regards football was tremendous. The discipline he had in getting ready for matches was really helpful to me as a younger player. It helped me blossom and achieve my potential. For all the young players at Derby to be involved with a professional like Dave Mackay was an unbelievable situation. He was inspirational, and it was a masterstroke by Cloughie in signing him to help the club grow. As a manager, although Brian liked clean sheets, Dave believed that if you could score one more than the opposition that was enough. Dave loved his teams to attack, and brought in Bruce Rioch as a midfielder who could score goals. So instead of maybe allowing the wingers to deal with it, Dave liked his midfield players to go on and score goals. His concept was if you had an attacking midfielder like Brucie playing alongside Archie Gemmill, it gave him a little bit more flexibility and strength in terms of attacking. With Archie covering every blade of grass, it allowed Brucie to push on and look for the knockdowns on the edge of the box, and then shoot from distance and often score spectacular goals.'

As a consequence of the games on 7 December, Stoke City confirmed their position as the First Division leaders, although just four points still covered the top eight teams. The Victoria Ground side won at Birmingham City, with three first-half goals, including a brace from Jimmy Greenhoff, eventually giving them an easy 3–0 victory. That success came on the day that the Stoke boss Tony Waddington received the 'Manager of the Month' award for November, his side having lost just one of their previous six League fixtures. There were plenty of goals elsewhere in the division: Burnley, Middlesbrough and Tottenham Hotspur also enjoyed 3–0 wins, their respective victories coming against Queen's Park Rangers, Ipswich Town and Newcastle United. In all, the 11 First Division games produced a healthy total of 33 goals. In the Second Division, although Sheffield Wednesday and Manchester United shared eight goals at Hillsborough, an excellent contest was ruined by another bout of hooliganism. The visiting supporters invaded the pitch as the game progressed, and were only repelled by the use of police officers on horseback.

The following day, almost 100 managers met in Coventry to discuss a number of current issues within the game. One topic given an airing was that of defensive walls at free-kicks, something that had become an increasingly poorly handled refereeing decision over the opening months of the season. Also, in a testament to the changing nature of football, the meeting was addressed by Sir Jack Scamp, an industrialist and expert on contract law. The introduction of a policy giving freedom within a contract was something the Professional Footballers' Association, led by the soon-to-retire Wolverhampton Wanderers player Derek Dougan, were keen to see implemented as a replacement for the traditional retain and transfer system.

Buoyed by their performance at Anfield, the Rams set out to face Velez Mostar in the second leg of their UEFA Cup tie. Following the club's participation in the 1973 European Cup, the game against the Yugoslavians represented a seventh journey to foreign soil – one that proved, however, to be anything but seventh time lucky. For the seasoned band of Rams fans who had made trips to experience the delights of capital cities such as Lisbon, Rome and most recently Madrid, the bright December sunshine of the Adriatic coastal resort of Dubrovnik provided the only pleasant memory of their visit to the Balkans. The Rams crashed to a 4–1 defeat in a controversial game, with the away goal that Velez had scored at the Baseball Ground meaning that they progressed to the next stage of the competition on a 5–4 aggregate.

11 December 1974
UEFA Cup 3rd Round – 2nd Leg
Velez Mostar 4 v Derby County 1
(aggregate 5–4)

Late penalty ends Rams' European dreams...

After defeating Velez Mostar 3–1 at the Baseball Ground, Dave Mackay had warned his players that 'the tie was far from over'. Those words came back to haunt him at the tiny Gradski Stadium when the Yugoslavs, thanks to an inspired first-half display and a late disputed penalty, eliminated the Rams from the competition on aggregate.

The Velez pre-match hopes were given a huge boost when Bajavic, their World Cup player with 32 international caps, reported fit after a long absence. His return, along with the performance of fellow Yugoslavian international Vladic, turned the contest in favour of the home team, their efforts being appreciated by a noisy crowd of 15,000 who throughout the contest discharged a barrage of fireworks into the night sky. The Rams manager had hoped that an away goal would be enough to see his side progress, but he could not have envisaged that the Rams would concede three within the space of a little more than 50 minutes.

The visitors looked nervous from the outset, their state of mind contributing to the first goal. In the 12th minute, Archie Gemmill failed to clear a half-hit shot from Bajavic, and in his frantic efforts to win back the ball he brought down Vukoje. The referee pointed to the penalty spot, Primorac driving the spot kick into the net despite Colin Boulton getting his hand to the ball. Worse was to follow for the Rams. On the half-hour, a corner from Vladic was punched out by Boulton – the ball travelling to the edge of the penalty area where Pecejl, after a neat piece of control, fired it back through the crowd of players and into the net. It levelled the contest on a 3–3 aggregate, with the Velez goal in Derby giving them the advantage.

On an uneven surface, the Rams found it difficult to exert any real control over the proceedings, their frustration being exemplified by bookings for Kevin Hector and Peter Daniel. Within minutes of the second half starting, the home side went further ahead with Vladic again involved. Colin Todd gave away a free-kick 25 yards from goal, and the influential midfielder blasted in a shot which cruelly went in off Boulton's back – the goalkeeper having initially managed to divert the effort onto the underside of the bar. After his recent utilisation of substitutes, Mackay had developed something of a 'Midas touch'. He replaced Jeff Bourne with Roger Davies after 55 minutes, his ploy again reaping an immediate reward. Two minutes later, Henry Newton delivered a cross from the left, and Davies headed the ball down for Hector to nip between two defenders to score. After conceding a goal, just had they had done at the Baseball Ground, Velez began to panic and Newton could have won the game twice within a few minutes. He hit the post with a thunderbolt 20-yard shot, which was followed by another fierce drive that just cleared the bar. Then, after Alan Hinton had replaced Francis Lee in the 73rd minute, a corner from the second replacement fell to Hector, who saw his shot kicked off the line.

At 4–4 and with extra time beckoning, the game was decided by Mr Corver. There were four minutes left when a shot from Vujoke hit Todd on the shoulder from a distance of no more than three yards. The referee indicated that the Rams defender had used his hand to bring the ball down… and the resulting penalty was slammed home by the returning hero Bajavic. It was a far from satisfactory way for the Rams to exit the competition, their fightback thwarted by what appeared to be a very dubious refereeing decision.

Velez Mostar: Mrgan, Meter, Hadziabdic, Colic, Primorac, Pecejl, Topic, Hallhodzic, Bajavic, Vladic, Vukoje. Substitutes: None used.

Derby County: Boulton, Webster, Thomas, Rioch, Daniel, Todd, Newton, Gemmill, Bourne, Hector, Lee. Substitutes: Davies for Bourne (55), Hinton for Lee (73).

Attendance: 15,000
Referee: Mr Corver (Holland)
Post-match positions: n/a

The manner of the defeat incensed Mackay, and the Rams manager became embroiled in a post-match bust-up with the Dutch referee. He certainly left reporters in no doubt about his feelings: 'We have been cheated out of this game and out of Europe – and the man who cheated us is the referee.' Without requesting that the match be replayed, on their return to Britain the Rams protested to UEFA about what they saw as the official's poor behaviour and lapses in concentration. Their case centred on the fact that Mr Corver had allowed the contest to proceed in a hail of fireworks from the terraces, something that UEFA had strictly forbidden, and also that Francis Lee had been, rather bizarrely, allowed to kick off in both halves of the game. The length of time taken to resolve the Rams' case bordered on the farcical. After initially including both teams in the draw for the next round, UEFA took until the middle of February 1975 to announce that the Rams' appeal had been dismissed.

Mackay's despondent mood was not improved by the news that Kevin Hector was facing a rare spell on the sidelines. The Rams striker, who remarkably had not missed a game since the visit of Manchester City on 4 November 1972, suffered damage to his knee ligaments late on in the Velez game, and was immediately ruled out of the the matches either side of Christmas. With David Nish also still on the treatment table and McFarland struggling to regain fitness, there was a general air of gloom surrounding the Baseball Ground ahead of the visit of Everton on 14 December. Interestingly, the fixture was sponsored by Gillette, with the company, better known for its support of cricket, experiencing a first commercial taste of the winter game. Supporters attending the match also enjoyed two pre-kick-off presentations: Francis Lee received the *Daily Mirror* 'Footballer of the Month' award for November, and the newly-crowned British bantamweight champion boxer Dave Needham paraded his Lonsdale belt.

In domestic midweek games, Newcastle recovered from a first-leg defeat by Southampton to win the Texaco Cup 3–1 on aggregate at St James' Park, the visitors not being helped by the dismissal of Jim Steele. It was the second successive year that the Magpies had won the competition.

14 December 1974
Football League Division One
Derby County 0 v Everton 1

Rams fail to overcome cynical Everton...

Everton emerged victorious from what was essentially a poor quality contest. The visitors gained few new friends, however, their success being based on a display of ruthless tackling which at times threatened to spill over into outright violence. Although the two points lifted the Merseyside club to the top of the First Division, most devotees of good football hoped that they would be overtaken before the conclusion of the campaign.

After the disappointment of their result in Yugoslavia, the game completed a bad few days for the Rams, the scoreline representing their sixth League defeat of the season. Derby had plenty of opportunities to win the game within the opening 30 minutes. Francis Lee hit the bar with a superb piece of individual skill early on, and Roger Davies was foiled by a diving save from Dai Davies after a powerful burst into the penalty area. Archie Gemmill, again thriving in the atmosphere of a hard-fought encounter, was frequently targeted as the playmaker the Toffees needed to restrict. As a consequence, Everton seemed content to give away plenty of free-kicks, and on two occasions Bruce Rioch came close to punishing their indiscretions. He smashed both efforts goalwards, but Davies managed to divert the shots over the bar. In one of the worst tackles of the afternoon, Gemmill was also the victim of a crude lunge at his thigh from Roger Kenyon, which surprisingly went unpunished by the referee. In the 10 minutes before half-time, things almost went beyond the official's control. George Telfer and David Jones were booked within a minute of each other, their cautions following an earlier booking for the rugged Mike Lyons.

Having defied the Rams for 45 minutes, at least Everton attempted to play more constructively after the interval. Indeed, they could have gone ahead when Peter Daniel conceded a free-kick, in a dangerous position, just outside the penalty area. Jones took the kick and blasted in a shot, which Colin Boulton managed to fingertip away. At the other end, from another free-kick, Lee drove his shot off the four-man wall, but frustratingly the ball again hit the crossbar and spun to safety.

Everton broke the deadlock in the 65th minute. Jones picked up the ball in midfield and floated a cross to the far post. As the Rams defence went walkabout, Bob Latchford, in acres of space, headed past Boulton and in off the post. Derby responded, but despite their honest endeavours, the visitors' back four held firm, thanks to a mixture of physical challenges and solid organisation. Dave Clements emerged as their best defender. Colin Todd, meanwhile, was selected as the sponsors' 'Man of the Match' after yet another magnificent display.

Dave Mackay promised his side 'would be back'. However, despite Todd's continued excellence, the goal was the 30th the Rams had conceded in 21 games. When they won the Championship in 1972, Brian Clough's team gave up just 33 over the whole campaign.

Derby County: Boulton, Webster, Thomas, Rioch, Daniel, Todd, Newton, Gemmill, Davies, Bourne, Lee. Substitute: Hinton for Bourne (73).

Everton: Davies, Bernard, Seargeant, Clements, Kenyon, Hurst, Jones, Telfer, Lyons, Latchford, Connolly. Substitute: Pearson for Telfer (77).

Attendance: 24,991

Referee: Mr Spencer

Post-match positions: Derby 9, Everton 1

On 18 December, Steve Powell made his debut for the England Under-23 team in their 3–0 defeat of Scotland at Aberdeen. It was a brief bright spot in what proved to be a frustrating season for the Rams midfielder. Having sat on the bench throughout an earlier international, Powell had played superbly as the replacement for Colin Todd, but found himself back on reserve-team duty once the defender had recovered from his groin operation. England's comfortable win north of the border was overshadowed by the absence from the England team of Kevin Beattie, the Ipswich player preferring to spend some time in his native Cumbria rather than join up with the rest of the squad. Beattie additionally missed the Ipswich 1–0 victory at Leicester City on 20 December, a contest which saw another player, Keith Weller, also catapulted into the headlines for all the wrong reasons.

Weller staged a one-man protest at the decision of the Leicester board not to allow him a transfer. He refused to go back onto the pitch for the second half of the match, and had left the ground when the other players came in at the end. His actions cost him a club fine of two weeks' wages, but Weller was placed on the transfer list, a request that was subsequently withdrawn. Many other managers were, however, stunned that a professional player could take such a stance, and several, led by John Bond of Norwich City, demanded that the midfielder be blacklisted and forced to stay at Leicester.

With the Rams' interest in the UEFA Cup effectively over, Mackay used the period before Christmas to rally his troops for a concerted effort over the second half of the season. He set them a target of 33 points from their remaining 21 games, a schedule that would produce an end of season total of 56, enough, he anticipated, to win the League. However, in light of their subsequent performance at Luton (see report), the Rams boss was forced to issue the following ultimatum: 'Improve or face the consequences, the current level of achievement is not acceptable.' It was a hard-hitting blast aimed at the entire squad. Mackay's message was clear enough – his sights were firmly set on improving on the third-place finish of the previous season.

In the midweek domestic games, the quarter-finals of the League Cup were finally decided, three of the four ties being settled after a replay. Manchester United, Chester and Norwich joined Aston Villa at the semi-final stage – Villa, with a 2–1 win at Colchester United, being the only side to proceed at the first opportunity.

21 December 1974
Football League Division One
Luton Town 1 v Derby County 0

Second win for Hatters as Rams create little...

Luton Town gained just their second League win of the season after a woeful display by Derby County at Kenilworth Road. Against a side which handed them control of the midfield area from the outset, the Rams struggled to pose any real concerns for the home defenders, the Hatters including the former Burton Albion defender Steve Buckley at left-back. Dave Mackay named the same team that had lost to Everton, Kevin Hector being absent for a second successive League match for the first time since 1967. He was certainly missed, with Jeff Bourne in particular looking unable to fathom a way past the frequently packed home defence.

The initial play was untidy with neither side looking comfortable in the wet and windy conditions. Francis Lee managed to create space for himself on a couple of occasions in the first half, but the Luton goalkeeper Graham Horn was not called upon to make anything resembling a serious save. Although the interval arrived with the game scoreless, the Rams' percentage of the possession was so high that a goal seemed certain after the break.

ROD THOMAS

Things did not improve, however, and time after time the visitors gave the ball away in good positions. Indeed, it was only after the arrival of Alan Hinton on the hour that Luton came under any significant pressure. The left-winger started to supply a number of accurately lofted centres, but unfortunately the fact that Roger Davies, the one player who could have made best use of Hinton's accuracy, had been withdrawn largely negated the substitute's contribution. The contest was settled by a penalty in the 81st minute. Peter Spiring, a recent £60,000 addition from Liverpool, attacked on the left and was fouled by Colin Todd . Despite Colin Boulton's dive, Jim Ryan's crisp spot-kick went into the net, the crowd of just under 13,000 erupting at the prospect of a rare success.

It was an altogether unsatisfactory performance from the Rams. Their assistant manager Des Anderson seemed bemused by what he had witnessed. 'There must be some sort of mental block,' he told reporters. 'We made no impact on this game, none at all.' Fortunately, with the other results going in their favour, the Rams remained just five points behind the leaders Ipswich Town – the East Anglians taking over the top position on goal difference from Everton and Manchester City, with a 1–0 win at Leicester City.

Luton Town: Horn, Ryan, Buckley, Anderson, Faulkner, Futcher, Ryan, Husband, Spiring, West, Aston. Substitute: Fuccillo for Spiring (81).

Derby County: Boulton, Webster, Thomas, Rioch, Daniel, Todd, Newton, Gemmill, Davies, Bourne, Lee. Substitute: Hinton for Davies (60).

Attendance: 12,862
Referee: Mr Lees

Post-match positions: Derby 10, Luton 22

26 December 1974
Football League Division One
Derby County 2 v Birmingham City 1

Inspired Gemmill steers Rams to victory...

After stumbling to defeat against Everton and Luton, the Rams bounced back to form with a well-deserved victory over Birmingham – gaining therefore a measure of revenge for the controversial loss they had suffered at St Andrews in September. With Kevin Hector still on the sidelines, Dave Mackay stayed loyal to the front three who had failed to score in the previous two matches. Elsewhere for the Rams, David Nish came through a late fitness test and returned at left-back ahead of Rod Thomas. It was also a very special day for Ron Webster. He was presented with a silver salver after the game to mark his 500th appearance for the club. The Belper-born full-back had served the Rams magnificently over the seasons, his consistency earning him the tag of 'Mr Reliable', so rarely had the popular defender let his teammates down.

On another notoriously difficult Baseball Ground surface, the Rams had much the better of the early play. Although Dave Latchford, the Birmingham shot-stopper, impressed with a couple of saves from Roger Davies, he had little chance with the opening goal. After 37 minutes Davies, after a neat piece of control, got clear on the right wing, and his low centre was converted by Jeff Bourne. The wily Francis Lee also contributed significantly by allowing the ball to run through to Bourne, a deft move which totally deceived his marker Malcolm Page and set up the easiest of finishes.

The opener was nothing more than Derby deserved, but they could have gone behind moments earlier. Kenny Burns got clear and was only halted by a Webster challenge which conceded a free-kick. In the absence of ruptured knee victim Trevor Francis, Burns looked to be the most dangerous Birmingham forward, but Peter Daniel again demonstrated his worth and coped well with the aerial threat posed by the combative Scot. After the interval, Burns became increasingly frustrated and, after another move had broken down, kicked out at Colin Todd. Despite the fact that the defender responded with a left hook, both men went unpunished by the generally lenient Mr Lee.

The Rams' second goal in the 65th minute was a magnificent effort. Bruce Rioch picked up a loose ball on the edge of the penalty area, exchanged passes with Lee, and then thrashed a drive past Latchford from a narrow angle. Rioch often frustrated supporters with a lack of involvement, but his ability to produce an occasional flash of brilliance made him a potential match-winner. Colin Boulton, who had handled well throughout, was only denied a clean sheet deep into injury time. Jim Calderwood delivered a hopeful cross and, after Bourne had fluffed his clearance, Bob Hatton nipped in to score the Blues' consolation goal.

The two best players on the pitch opposed each other in midfield. Archie Gemmill again covered an enormous amount of ground, his guile and enthusiasm being matched by Howard Kendall, who again looked to be a high-class performer.

Derby County: Boulton, Webster, Nish, Daniel, Todd, Newton, Gemmill, Davies, Bourne, Lee. Substitute: Hinton.

Birmingham City: Latchford, Page, Styles, Kendall, Gallagher, Pendrey, Campbell, Taylor, Burns, Hatton, Calderwood. Substitute: Hendrie.

Attendance: 26,121
Referee: Mr Lee
Post-match positions: Derby 10, Birmingham 15

28 December 1974
Football League Division One
Manchester City 1 v Derby County 2

Super Franny punishes City...

Just 48 hours after dispensing with Birmingham City, the Rams thrust themselves right back into the race for the Championship. In a game of fine football and even finer goals, they emerged from Maine Road with both points, ending the Blues' previously unbeaten sequence of 12 home games. The day was a personal triumph for Francis Lee, who was facing his former employers for the first time. Having refused to get involved in the pre-match speculation concerning his appearance, Franny stole the show and netted the winning goal with a fabulous second-half strike. Although Lee was a giant for the visitors, Henry Newton also produced a rare goal and a superb performance – certainly his best of of the campaign.

City had given up just six goals at home before this encounter, but they fell behind as early as the 21st minute. Bruce Rioch knocked in a centre and, although the ball was cleared, Newton headed it back in to Lee and was on hand to strike the return pass into the top corner. As the home side threatened an immediate response, the Rams midfield was seen at its best. Rioch and Archie Gemmill worked tirelessly and Newton won a series of important tackles around the edge of his own penalty area. The few times that the visitors' back four was breached, Colin Boulton remained sharp and saved well from Dennis Tueart and Mike Doyle, his diving stop from Doyle's header at a corner being particularly impressive.

In the second half City pressed again, and their deserved equaliser came in the 63rd minute. It was a marvellously crafted effort and demonstrated the exciting potential of Tony Book's side. Asa Hartford and Rodney Marsh linked perfectly in a darting move in from the left flank, and Colin Bell, in full stride, hit a screaming

Lee tangles with former teammate Alan Oakes during the 2–1 win at Maine Road. Oakes's nephew Andy would later play in goal at Pride Park for the Rams.

first-time shot past Boulton. The reply from Derby was immediate, and amazingly they netted a goal of equal quality within two minutes. A move, instigated by David Nish, saw the ball slipped inside to Lee, who had his back to goal. In a flash the Rams striker turned inside and past Alan Oakes – and then smashed a rising 30-yard shot past the hapless Joe Corrigan into the far top corner. It was a superb goal against the club who had rejected him. The added irony of the afternoon's events was that Joe Royle, signed for £200,000 from Everton on Christmas Eve as a 'goalscorer', made a very subdued home debut.

The City manager acknowledged the Rams' display and was not critical of his own team's efforts. 'We played better than we have for three or four weeks,' he told reporters. Lee, meanwhile, described the goal as a 'Roy of the Rovers' experience.

Manchester City: Corrigan, Hammond, Donachie, Bell, Doyle, Oakes, Horswill, Royle, Marsh, Hartford, Tueart. Substitute: Henson.

Derby County: Boulton, Webster, Nish, Rioch, Daniel, Todd, Newton, Gemmill, Davies, Bourne, Lee. Substitute: Hinton.

Attendance: 40,188

Referee: Mr Gow

Post-match positions: Derby 9, Manchester City 8

Lee's goal and celebration were recorded by the *Match of the Day* cameras. The quality of the strike was such that, 30 years later, it regularly gets included in any retrospective programme that includes action from the mid-seventies. Barry Davies also played his part as the BBC commentator on the match: 'Lee... interesting... very interesting... Look at his face, just look at his face!' he exclaimed to millions of Saturday night viewers – as Lee wheeled away after scoring with an expression of total delight. The phrase stuck in the minds of Rams fans, and *Interesting, very interesting* later became the name of a Derby County fanzine.

The victory moved the Rams up to end the year in ninth place, with a total of 27 points from their opening 24 League fixtures. The top of the table remained incredibly congested, and Ipswich moved back to first place after a 1–0 victory over Birmingham, although their 30-point tally was matched by Middlesbrough. The nature of the season was reflected in the fact that Ipswich headed the table despite their wins at Filbert Street and St Andrews ending a miserable sequence of seven consecutive away defeats. The Portman Road club had also suffered a Boxing Day reversal at home to Luton Town – a contest which saw the controversial referee Mr Nippard needing to be given a police escort off the pitch after disallowing Bobby Robson's men a 'goal'.

Indeed, while the standings demonstrated what a tight campaign was developing, they also revealed one of the major differences between the First Division of the mid-seventies and the modern Premiership. On 28 December during the 1974–75 season, the top 14 teams were separated by just six points. The strongest reason for this was that 30 years ago, clubs were more evenly matched, and, on a given day, especially at home, the majority of teams were capable of beating each other. In contrast, a glance at the Premiership at Christmas 2003 – with its financial 'haves' and 'have nots' – reveals that although Manchester United topped the table (on an adjusted two points for a win basis) with 31 points, the 14th-placed team Blackburn Rovers had just 15 points, a much larger points spread of 16.

Division One – 28 December 1974

		P	W	D	L	GF	GA	PTS
1	Ipswich Town	25	14	2	9	34	19	30
2	Middlesbrough	25	11	8	6	37	28	30
3	Liverpool	23	12	5	6	34	20	29
4	Everton	24	8	13	3	33	25	29
5	Stoke City	25	11	7	7	39	33	29
6	West Ham United	25	10	8	7	42	33	28
7	Burnley	25	11	6	8	45	40	28
8	Manchester City	25	11	6	8	31	33	28
9	**Derby County**	**24**	**10**	**7**	**7**	**38**	**33**	**27**
10	Newcastle United	23	10	6	7	33	31	26
11	Leeds United	25	10	5	10	35	30	25
12	Wolverhampton Wdrs	24	8	9	7	32	30	25
13	Queen's Park Rangers	25	10	5	10	32	33	25
14	Sheffield United	24	9	6	9	31	36	24
15	Coventry City	25	7	9	9	33	41	23
16	Birmingham City	25	9	4	12	35	39	22
17	Tottenham Hotspur	25	7	7	11	30	35	21
18	Chelsea	24	6	9	9	26	41	21
19	Arsenal	24	7	6	11	28	30	20
20	Carlisle United	25	7	3	15	25	33	17
21	Leicester City	24	5	6	13	22	37	16
22	Luton Town	24	4	7	13	22	37	15

CHAPTER SIX
January 1975

Todd saves Rams' blushes with rare goals...

In the majority of their games before the turn of the year, the Rams' best player was Colin Todd. Week after week, almost every Sunday morning match report described his performance as 'magnificent' or 'exceptional' – such was the prowess of the central defender. Against Orient, Todd again duly claimed the headlines, but this time his two goals saved Derby County from certain defeat. The Second Division side belied their 15th place standing for long periods, and sensationally were 2–0 ahead within the first quarter of an hour. Credit then had to go to the Rams for fighting back, but this was definitely not the start to the New Year that Dave Mackay had envisaged.

With Kevin Hector back in training, but not considered fit enough to return to the action, the Rams were unchanged with Alan Hinton on the substitutes' bench, awaiting a chance to mark his 300th appearance for the club. Although the opening exchanges were even enough, they gave no indication of what was to follow. In the 13th minute Todd – on his 200th appearance for the club – conceded a free-kick and Phil Hoadley floated in a centre from the right. Colin Boulton attempted to punch the ball to safety, but it eventually fell to Derek Possee, who hit a superb shot into the net. Two minutes later it was 2–0 to the London side. Hoadley lofted a long pass into the heart of the Rams defence and, after Possee had headed on, Gerry Queen, the former Crystal Palace striker, shot high into the net from the edge of the penalty area.

Derby made hard work of disposing of Orient in the FA Cup third round. Here O's keeper John Jackson thwarts Roger Davies in the first game at Brisbane Road.

For the remainder of the half Orient remained the better team. Their defence, tight and controlled, held up Francis Lee and Roger Davies well – and indeed the nearest the Rams came to scoring was when David Nish forced John Jackson to save a free-kick. However, with the interval beckoning, Archie Gemmill squared a free-kick to Todd, who from 30 yards out blasted in a shot, albeit off the leg of

Derek Downing, which went beyond Jackson. It was his first goal since October 1972 when he scored against Sheffield United at the Baseball Ground.

After the break, and no doubt with the harsh words of Mackay echoing around their ears, the Rams looked much more positive and their attacks had a greater purpose. However, for all of their effort, Orient held firm and could have gone further ahead – Mr Crabb waving aside their claims for a 73rd-minute penalty when Possee went down under a challenge from Ron Webster. The equaliser eventually came with seven minutes remaining. Todd knocked up a pass to Bruce Rioch, who charged forward and cut inside from the flank. Todd, meanwhile, with time against the Rams, continued his run and when Rioch's return pass arrived, he drove the ball home – second time around with the slightest of deflections off Davies.

At the final whistle the Rams, given their overall display, were fortunate to escape with a replay. That said, many a successful cup run in previous years had started with a generous slice of luck.

Orient: Jackson, Fisher, Downing, Allen, Hoadley, Walley, Fairbrother, Bennett, Queen, Grealish, Possee. Substitute: Cunningham.

Derby County: Boulton, Webster, Nish, Rioch, Daniel, Todd, Newton, Gemmill, Davies, Bourne, Lee. Substitute: Hinton for Bourne (63).

Attendance: 12,490
Referee: Mr Crabb

Post-match positions: n/a

Thirty years on, Roy McFarland made the following assessment of Todd's overall contribution:

'In one way, Colin Todd's performance at Orient in the FA Cup typified how awesome he was that season. We were losing 2–0 and Toddy came up and scored two great goals. Without me, he had the responsibility at the back and he took the mantle and held the team together. Colin was the crux of the success. Peter [Daniel] wasn't a regular in our side but Toddy gelled with him, cajoled him and for me was outstanding, the main man'.

On the eve of the third round of the FA Cup – one of the most eagerly awaited days of the season – Second Division Nottingham Forest sacked their manager Allan Brown. Forest had struggled from the outset of the campaign and, without the services of ace marksman Duncan McKenzie, had won just nine of their opening 25 League games and stood in 13th place in the table. Within 48 hours of Brown's departure, Brian Clough had been unveiled as the new manager at the City Ground. It was, of course, an appointment which was to ultimately herald the start of the most successful period of club management in the history of the British game.

With McFarland unable to resume playing, the Rams captaincy remained with Archie Gemmill, who had responded well to the additional burden placed upon him. By his own admission, it was a not a role the midfielder had taken on naturally, as he revealed after the first couple of months of the campaign. 'At the start of the season, instead of thinking about my own game, I was wondering what everyone else was doing – instead of trusting them to get on with their own jobs.' From October onwards, however, Gemmill certainly put those early concerns behind him, and excelled in many of the Rams' fixtures – notably in the victories achieved on the energy-sapping Baseball Ground surface. Indeed, at the time only one topic still riled the patriotic Paisley-born Scot – his absence from Willie Ormond's national team. 'It's an immense disappointment to me, especially as I feel that I am at my peak. The manager has looked at a number of new players this season, but has not seen me play once – I can only assume that I do not currently feature in his plans,' Gemmill said.

8 January 1975
Football Association Cup – 3rd Round replay
Derby County 2 v Orient 1

Last-gasp Rioch keeps Rams in the Cup...

The Rams eventually progressed to the fourth round of the FA Cup but they certainly made hard work of overcoming a spirited Orient side who, just as they had done in the opening game, looked the better team for much of the contest. In their defence, Derby did have to readjust after an enforced substitution: Ron Webster injured his knee in the 13th minute and limped off before the half-hour to be replaced by Alan Hinton.

Anybody arriving slightly late to the game would have missed the opening goals. In the fourth minute, a long lofted ball from Tom Walley allowed Barry Fairbrother to run clear and plant a shot past Colin Boulton from just inside the penalty area. The Rams' response was immediate. Colin Todd, the hero at Brisbane Road, burst forward from defence and fed Jeff Bourne with a neat pass. Bourne reacted well and delivered in a low centre which Francis Lee easily side-footed past John Jackson – it was his 14th goal of the season.

Much of what followed was spoiled by the heavily sanded pitch, which in places made good football impossible. The arrival of Hinton did at least give the Rams more options out wide, but although both Lee and Bourne had good chances blocked, the central strikers again found themselves restricted by the no-nonsense defending of Phil Hoadley and Walley. With the visitors dangerous whenever they broke clear, the Rams could again have gone in behind at the interval. Derek Possee worked a chance for himself, but Boulton dived bravely to save at the striker's feet. After the break, Orient again looked lively, especially with the introduction of their speedy teenager Laurie Cunningham, who seemed capable of worrying the Rams defence whenever he received the ball. As Dave Mackay's side eventually rallied, Bourne did have the ball in the net, but the referee had already decided that Lee had committed a foul on the excellent Hoadley. Orient's last major chance came in the 70th minute, when Boulton was forced to rush out and block a shot from Fairbrother.

It took a moment of rare skill to settle the tie – and deny the London side the chance of extra-time. In the 88th minute, David Nish advanced up the left flank and exchanged passes with Roger Davies. The full-back then pulled the ball back into the path of Bruce Rioch, who hammered a shot past Jackson from 20 yards out. Again, largely out of the action for the majority of the game, Rioch silenced his critics with a match-winning goal – impressively for a midfielder, his 12th of the campaign.

A relieved Rams manager emerged to breathe a sigh of relief at the end. 'See you in the next round' he quipped to reporters, his major concern from the game being the extent of Webster's problems – the right-back had looked badly injured when he came off.

Derby County: Boulton, Webster, Nish, Rioch, Daniel, Todd, Newton, Gemmill, Davies, Bourne, Lee. Substitute: Hinton for Webster (27).

Orient: Jackson, Fisher, Downing, Allen, Hoadley, Walley, Fairbrother, Bennett, Queen, Grealish, Possee. Substitute: Cunningham for Bennett (45).

Attendance: 26,501
Referee: Mr Crabb
Post-match positions: n/a

The Rams were not alone in struggling to overcome opponents from a lower division. Indeed, the third round generated more shocks than normal, with all of the remaining five non-League sides producing excellent performances. The major surprise came at Turf Moor, where Burnley were defeated 1–0 by Wimbledon, then in the Southern League. Leatherhead,

Rod Thomas, the Welsh international full-back, had been signed by Mackay from Swindon Town, with a view to replacing Ron Webster in November 1973. By January 1975 Webster was still keeping Thomas out of the side, until injury let him in. Thomas then had a run in the team, playing in most of the next hundred games before giving way himself to the emerging David Langan in 1976–77. Affectionately known on the terraces as 'Dyno-Rod', Thomas played in the last 18 games of the Championship run-in, only three of which were lost.

meanwhile, won by a similar scoreline against Brighton and Hove Albion, and Stafford Rangers beat Rotherham after a replay. Although both Altrincham and Wycombe Wanderers went out after replays against Everton and Middlesbrough, they both exited the competition with their heads held high, the south Manchester team in particular. Having held the Merseysiders to a 1–1 draw at Goodison, they attracted a crowd of over 35,000 to Old Trafford before the First Division team eventually beat them by two goals.

There were four all-First Division ties, each of which was decided at the first opportunity. Liverpool overcame Stoke City 2–0 at Anfield, while further north Newcastle defeated Manchester City by a similar margin. In the other two fixtures, Luton Town secured a fourth-round berth with a single-goal win at Birmingham City, and Ipswich Town overcame Wolverhampton Wanderers at Molineux by the odd goal in three.

With Ron Webster immediately ruled out for several games, Rod Thomas was given a chance to establish himself in his natural position. The Welsh international had only appeared in eight League games since his £80,000 transfer from Swindon Town and had waited patiently for a chance to demonstrate his true potential. For the visit of Liverpool, Dave Mackay also welcomed back Kevin Hector after an absence of six games, the Rams striker having regained full fitness after being injured against Velez Mostar on 11 December. With the Rams going into the weekend in ninth place, the fixture took on an added significance, although just six points still covered the top 14 clubs.

11 January 1975
Football League Division One
Derby County 2 v Liverpool 0

Hector returns to spark huge Rams victory...

The Rams were good value for this victory and, although Liverpool rallied after the interval, the final scoreline would have been greater had it not been for Ray Clemence. The Anfield goalkeeper produced several excellent saves, his point-blank reflex effort, late on, from David Nish being world class. The return of Kevin Hector seemed to galvanise the Rams attack, and the serial goalscorer was very unfortunate not to mark his comeback with a goal. The early exchanges went in favour of the visitors, with Kevin Keegan prompting a series of raids into the penalty area. The defence stood firm, however, with only a curling drive from Brian Hall causing Colin Boulton any significant problems – the Rams 'keeper responding with with a diving save. In fact, as the half progressed the home side came more into the contest and clearly looked happier on the heavily sanded surface. After the game, Bob Paisley cited the pitch as the main reason that his side had not gained at least a point. 'It was impossible to make three passes on the trot,' he told reporters. It was a genuine enough comment, and with nine of their remaining 15 fixtures being at home, the Rams' notorious pitch could have played a major role in determining the outcome of the Championship. Hector had already tested the visitors' offside trap before he beat it to set up the opening goal. Emlyn Hughes was left sprawling as Hector went past him, before passing to Henry Newton who netted with a crisp cross-shot beyond Clemence. It was the midfielder's second consecutive League goal, beautifully well taken and, given the calm assurance that he brought to the team from his role in front of the back four, a real bonus.

Liverpool came out revitalised after the interval, with John Toshack coming to prominence with his aerial threat. His clever touches enabled the visitors to create a number of chances – Boulton saving well from Keegan before Steve Heighway wasted a good opportunity to grab the equaliser. However, the Rams again soaked up the pressure well, and in the 80th minute Francis Lee ended the fight back. Peter Daniel set off on a run and his pass to Lee was converted with ease.

With the two points taking the Rams up to seventh place, Dave Mackay certainly had no doubts about the importance of the win. 'This was the most important game of our run in. Liverpool are the team we all have to beat,' he said. It was certainly a result that brought back memories of the Rams' triumph in 1972, when a victory in their last fixture against the Merseysiders gave them the chance to win the title.

Derby County: Boulton, Thomas, Nish, Rioch, Daniel, Todd, Newton, Gemmill, Davies, Hector, Lee. Substitute: Hinton.

Liverpool: Clemence, Neal, Lindsay, Thompson, Cormack, Hughes, Keegan, Hall, Heighway, Toshack, Callaghan. Substitute: Kennedy.

Attendance: 33,463

Referee: Mr Sinclair

Post-match positions: Derby 7, Liverpool 6

The attendance at the Baseball Ground was the best the Rams had achieved all season. The total was boosted by the presence of approximately 4,000 fervent Liverpool supporters, who ensured that there was a lively, but generally good humoured, atmosphere on the terraces. It was something that had been noticeably missing at many of the games in the first half of the campaign. After the match, the Rams players enjoyed a belated Christmas party in the town centre. The following morning, and no doubt with a few heavy heads, the squad flew out to Marbella for a five-day mid-season break. With the emphasis of the trip being on rest and relaxation rather than hard training, Webster stayed behind to receive further treatment to his knee. Lee, Todd and Daniel were all additionally excused from travelling for a variety of personal and business reasons.

Elsewhere in the games on 11 January, the most noticeable result came in the north-east, where Tottenham Hotspur defeated Newcastle 5–2 with Alfie Conn, on his first full appearance for the London club, netting a hat-trick. The Geordies had included recent signings Tommy Craig and Geoff Nulty in their line-up – the pair, together costing around £250,000, having been respectively purchased from Sheffield Wednesday and Burnley to cover an extensive pre-Christmas injury crisis. Ipswich maintained their position at the top with a 2–0 victory over Middlesbrough – their tally of 32 points being one more than Everton, who overcame Leicester City 3–0. With Luton's revival continuing with a point against Chelsea, that defeat for Leicester dropped them to bottom place in the standings with just 16 points. Leeds United beat West Ham United 2–1, the Yorkshire club being inspired by the return of Eddie Gray who was making his first League appearance of the season. The strangest incident of the day came at Bramall Lane in the game between Sheffield United and Manchester City. The referee, Mr Kirkpatrick, was forced to take the teams off the pitch in the second half while he made a loudspeaker appeal for a phantom whistler in the crowd to stop disrupting the play at critical moments.

18 January 1975
Football League Division One
Wolverhampton W 0 v Derby County 1

Newton strike enough to see off Wanderers...

This was a crucial victory for the Rams. Their single-goal success moved them up into fifth in the table, significantly just two points behind the leaders Everton. With the First Division remaining so complex, although the away win was only their fourth of the campaign, just Middlesbrough, Queen's Park Rangers and the table toppers had accumulated more points on their travels.

The match got off to an amazing start, and on another day Derby might have been behind, or perhaps even ahead within the opening minutes, as the chances came thick and fast at both ends. Colin Boulton saved with his legs from John Richards, that incident coming moments before Rod Thomas headed the ball off the line following a Steve Kindon header. For the Rams, Roger Davies nodded a right-sided throw-in into the path of Kevin Hector – but his sweetly hit volley came back off the bar with Phil Parkes well beaten.

Slowly but surely, the Rams midfield took control, with Archie Gemmill in superb form. As well as his incredible pitch coverage, he frequently and skillfully worked his way through with the ball to generate yet another opportunity. Indeed, it was the captain who set up the vital goal. In the 32nd minute, he linked up with Francis Lee, who was at the edge of the penalty area. Lee sensed Henry Newton's surge into the area and, although his pass was a little fast, the incoming midfielder got there ahead of two defenders and smashed home his shot as Parkes ventured towards him. It was Newton's third successive League goal, and his contribution became more important as the the season progressed. For the remainder of the half, the Rams' play was excellent. They stroked the ball around smoothly and Boulton was allowed the luxury of being a virtual spectator.

The home side, already with three straight defeats behind them, at least came out with more purpose after the break. They managed to create a couple of good chances, but Gemmill dived in bravely to block a drive from Kenny Hibbitt, and Richards shot wide after getting clear. As the game wore on, the Rams' composure grew, their performance a throwback to a vintage Brian Clough away win. Without necessarily needing to add to their advantage, they made sure that Wolves, and their supporters, became increasingly frustrated.

In defence, Colin Todd was again magnificent and snuffed out anything the home side created. Thomas, meanwhile, looked determined to finally lay claim to the right-back position. Nicely placed in the League and with an important Cup tie to come, Derby County returned home still the masters of their own destiny.

Wolverhampton Wanderers: Parkes, Palmer, Parkin, Bailey, Munroe, McAlle, Hibbitt, Dale, Richards, Kindon, Wagstaffe. Substitute: Powell for Palmer (57).

Derby County: Boulton, Thomas, Nish, Rioch, Daniel, Todd, Newton, Gemmill, Davies, Hector, Lee. Substitute: Powell.

Attendance: 24,516

Referee: Mr Hart

Post-match positions: Derby 5, Wolverhampton 14

In other League matches, Manchester City gained a quick revenge for their FA Cup exit against Newcastle – a hat-trick from Dennis Tueart easing them to a 5–1 success against the Geordies at Maine Road. Both of the Merseyside teams also maintained their challenge for the title: Liverpool won 2–1 against Coventry City, and Everton convincingly beat Birmingham City 3–0. After the weekend there was also a busy schedule of midweek fixtures. Colin Todd played the first half, as an over-age selection, in England's 2–0 victory over Wales at Under-23 level, and domestically the finalists for the League Cup were decided. After both semi-final first legs had produced 2–2 draws, Norwich City, thanks to a Colin Suggett header, beat Manchester United on a 3–2 aggregate. In the other game at Villa Park, two goals from Keith Leonard helped Aston Villa eventually overcome a spirited Chester side on a 5–4 aggregate.

With heavy rain affecting many areas of the country, the Rams fourth-round tie against Bristol Rovers was one of seven ties scheduled for 25 January which fell foul of the weather. With the Baseball Ground not known for its resilience to the extremes, it turned out to be a very simple task for Mr Jones of Ormskirk to call off the game as early as 9.15am and reschedule it for the Monday evening, thus giving the ground staff an immense amount of work to do to get the surface into a reasonable condition. In the games that did go ahead, Wimbledon again defied the odds by coming away from Elland Road with a scoreless draw against Leeds – the draw for the fifth round pairing the eventual winners with the Rams at the Baseball Ground. Leatherhead also seemed destined to produce another massive shock, but after establishing a 2–0 half-time advantage over Leicester City, they collapsed in the second period and were beaten 3–2. The third non-League team, Stafford Rangers, also exited the competition, the Northern Premier League club losing 2–1 at home against Peterborough United. In the other major Cup surprise Third Division Walsall beat Newcastle by a single goal, the Saddlers having earlier beaten Manchester United in the third round

27 January 1975
Football Association Cup 4th Round
Derby County 2 v Bristol Rovers 0

Rioch spot kick sees Rams home...

The Baseball Ground staff had worked all weekend to make the pitch playable for this rescheduled FA Cup tie, and their efforts were well rewarded as the Rams, with goals from Kevin Hector and Bruce Rioch, progressed to the fifth round at the expense of Bristol Rovers. In naming his side, Dave Mackay relied on the 11 that had defeated Wolverhampton Wanderers in the League. Colin Boulton thus setting a new appearance record for Derby County goalkeepers by playing in his 247th senior game. Despite all the work in getting the surface ready, the underfoot conditions still made good football very difficult. Fortunately, the Rams could usually rely on Archie Gemmill to thrive in the mud – and in this contest he was outstanding, his contribution matched only by the excellent Henry Newton, who was enjoying a rich vein of form. The home side took the lead in the 16th minute. Rod Thomas hurled an enormous long throw towards Roger Davies, and the centre-forward turned past a defender before crossing to the far post for Hector to score with ease. Thomas soon found himself involved at the other end of the pitch, with his beautifully timed tackle on Gordon Fearnley saving the

Rams' blushes after the Rovers man had gone clear. The Rams' riposte almost produced a second goal: Gemmill rounded the goalkeeper only to see his shot be kicked off the line, and David Nish curled a free-kick against the bar. In the second half, although the Rams had the majority of the possession, they failed to make the game safe, the visitors demonstrating admirable resistance with their Welsh Under-23 international defender Peter Aitken having a superb game.

Bristol Rovers were the next FA Cup opponents. Bruce Rioch despatched a trademark penalty past Jim Eadie in the Rams' 2–0 victory.

Bristol introduced David Staniforth into their attack with 12 minutes remaining, and the substitute almost immediately grabbed a bizarre equaliser. Colin Todd hit a back pass to Boulton, but the ball stuck in the mud. The Rams goalkeeper charged out to fly-kick the ball to safety, his clearance hitting Staniforth on the head and ballooning just over the bar. Much to the relief of the Rams supporters, the tie was finally settled in the 82nd minute. Gemmill exchanged passes with Rioch and was flattened by Frank Prince: Rioch placed the resulting penalty high and to the right of the goalkeeper. Jeff Bourne came on for the final few minutes, and after getting clear also saw a shot cleared of the line by Fearnley.

As the whistle sounded for full time, although the Rams had not played particularly well, they left the pitch safe in the knowledge that another home game awaited them in the fifth round.

Derby County: Boulton, Thomas, Nish, Rioch, Daniel, Todd, Newton, Gemmill, Davies, Hector, Lee. Substitute: Bourne for Lee (85).

Bristol Rovers: Eadie, Bater, Parsons, Aitken, Taylor, Prince, Stephens, Coombes, Warboys, Bannister, Fearnley. Substitute: Staniforth for Parsons (78).

Attendance: 27,980
Referee: Mr Jones

Post-match positions: n/a

Division One – 25 January 1975

		P	W	D	L	GF	GA	PTS
1	Everton	26	10	13	3	39	25	33
2	Ipswich Town	27	15	2	10	37	21	32
3	Burnley	27	13	6	8	47	40	32
4	Liverpool	25	13	5	7	36	23	31
5	**Derby County**	**26**	**12**	**7**	**7**	**41**	**33**	**31**
6	Middlesbrough	27	11	9	7	37	30	31
7	Stoke City	27	11	9	7	40	34	31
8	Manchester City	27	12	7	8	37	35	31
9	Leeds United	27	12	5	10	39	31	29
10	West Ham United	27	10	9	8	45	37	29
11	Sheffield United	26	10	7	9	35	38	27
12	Queen's Park Rangers	27	10	6	11	34	36	26
13	Newcastle United	25	10	6	9	36	41	26
14	Wolverhampton Wdrs	26	8	9	9	33	33	25
15	Coventry City	27	8	9	10	36	44	25
16	Arsenal	26	8	7	11	30	31	23
17	Tottenham Hotspur	27	8	7	12	36	40	23
18	Birmingham City	27	9	5	13	35	42	23
19	Chelsea	26	6	10	10	27	44	22
20	Carlisle United	27	8	3	16	28	36	19
21	Leicester City	26	5	7	14	23	41	17
22	Luton Town	26	4	8	14	23	39	16

CHAPTER SEVEN

February

1 February 1975
Football League Division One
Queen's Park Rangers 4 v Derby County 1

Rams foiled by late late Rangers...

The final scoreline at Loftus Road did not reflect the overall balance of the game. For 80 minutes the Rams matched Rangers in an absorbing contest but, after a disputed second goal, the home side ended with a flourish and added two more. With Ron Webster still out after the FA Cup replay with Orient, Rod Thomas continued at right-back for Derby. Rangers, meanwhile, included Don Masson in their line-up, the former Notts County man having inspired the Londoners to collect nine points from their previous six games.

Dave Mackay's season-long promise that the Rams would entertain away from home was demonstrated from the kick-off. His side opened at a frenzied pace and went ahead within the space of three minutes with a marvellous goal from Bruce Rioch. It was the Scottish international's 14th strike of the season, and as good as any he had scored – charging in to smash a loose ball past Phil Parkes from 25 yards. The explosive start to the game was maintained when Rangers levelled the proceedings just six minutes later. Masson delicately floated in a free-kick which deceived Peter Daniel and allowed Don Givens to hit a cross-shot towards the net, the ball going in off the retreating David Nish, although the strike was

An unusual picture taken during the defeat at Loftus Road. Bruce Rioch is tackled by the home side's Ian Gillard with Colin Todd in close attendance, but look closely at the lettering on Derby's shirts. The Rams had taken the field in Queen's Park Rangers' change strip!

credited to the Rangers player. A clearly far from 100 percent fit Francis Lee came off after just 16 minutes, but the enforced change did not unduly disrupt the Rams' flow. For the remainder of the half both teams vied for the advantage, with both Archie Gemmill and Gerry Francis excelling on a muddy, strength-sapping surface.

As the second period wore on the Rams had the better chances. Roger Davies had a golden opportunity to restore the visitors' lead but, after getting clear of the last defender, his control let him down badly – Parkes made the rest look easy. With a draw looking to be the likely outcome, Rangers grabbed the lead in the 81st minute. A corner from Dave Thomas bobbled around in the Rams' penalty area before Givens lashed the ball past Colin Boulton. The defenders protested vigorously that the Eire international had scored from an offside position but, after consulting his linesman, Mr Jones allowed the goal to stand.

Derby struck back immediately and substitute Jeff Bourne hit the angle of the bar and post from a free-kick. It was not to be, however, and in the 87th minute Rangers went 3–1 ahead when John Beck neatly set up Thomas for his fourth goal of the season. Moments before the final whistle, a piece of magic from Stan Bowles set up Givens to complete his hat-trick with the easiest of chances. Rangers then took both points, the Rams finishing with nothing despite having produced, for long periods, their best away performance of the campaign.

Queen's Park Rangers: Parkes, Clement, Gillard, Masson, McLintock, Webb, Thomas, Francis, Beck, Bowles, Givens. Substitute: Leach.

Derby County: Boulton, Thomas, Nish, Rioch, Daniel, Todd, Newton, Gemmill, Davies, Hector, Lee. Substitute: Bourne for Lee (16).

Attendance: 20,686
Referee: Mr Jones

Post-match positions: Derby 8, Queen's Park Rangers 11

After the game, the Rangers manager Dave Sexton admitted that the visitors probably deserved the draw. 'I thought Derby would take a point, but we were able to catch them when they came out looking for an equaliser.' The setback was the Rams' first defeat in eight League and Cup games. Indeed, their form during January was further recognised when Dave Mackay was named as the First Division 'Manager of the Month' – the first time he had won the award. The Rams boss, whose favourite tipple was vodka, joked that he would raffle his bottle of Bells whisky among his players – adding with a smile that 'they can win me enough bottles to have one each'.

In the other fixtures affecting teams chasing the title, there were mixed fortunes for the two Merseyside clubs. Although a late goal from their substitute Jim Pearson gave Everton a single-goal success over Tottenham Hotspur at Goodison, their close neighbours Liverpool stumbled to a 2–0 defeat on their

An inspiration: Archie Gemmill, who took over the captaincy for the season following the injury to Roy McFarland. Gemmill was tremendous week after week and the creative hub of all the good things the Rams produced.

visit to Arsenal. At the Victoria Ground, meanwhile, Stoke City extended Manchester City's dismal run of away form, a brace from Ian Moores guiding the Potteries team to an impressive 4–0 victory. It was a result which had serious ramifications for the City goalkeeper Joe Corrigan. After revealing to reporters that he would rather quit the game rather than remain at Maine Road, the burly shot-stopper was fined and transfer-listed by the City manager Tony Book. Corrigan's outburst was prompted by his opinion that he was being blamed too much for the team's poor results, the Mancunians having won just one of their 14 away games, and having conceded 30 goals in the process.

On the international front, while the England manager Don Revie used the cancellation of the game against Cyprus to hold a four-day get-together for his squad, his Scottish counterpart Willie Ormond faced a more serious midweek challenge. The Scots travelled to Valencia for an important European Championship qualification game against Spain – and despite a goal from Joe Jordan, returned home disappointed to have only achieved a 1–1 draw.

8 February 1975
Football League Division One
Derby County 0 v Leeds United 0

Derby drop point in Baseball Ground stalemate...

Both defences held the whip hand in this encounter, Leeds ending as much the happier side with their share of the spoils. Dave Mackay named an unchanged Rams team, although Archie Gemmill was playing his last game before commencing a two-game suspension after accumulating 12 disciplinary points. Neither John

Dave Mackay liked to attack but sometimes Derby needed to defend as well.
Here is a wall of players crucial to the Championship success.

From left to right: Rod Thomas, Bruce Rioch, Kevin Hector, Henry Newton, Archie Gemmill and Francis Lee.

O'Hare nor John McGovern was included in the visitors' 11, and the Leeds manager Jimmy Armfield was also without Norman Hunter, who was recuperating from a cartilage operation.

Leeds looked the stronger side in the opening minutes, but despite their pressure the Rams defence held firm and Colin Boulton was not required to make a significant save. As the half progressed the balance of the contest changed and, with Gemmill in excellent form, it was the visitors who were required to defend. The first real chance fell to Francis Lee, who took a pass from Colin Todd before firing in a tremendous shot which David Harvey managed to turn away for a corner. The Leeds goalkeeper also did well to stop a drive from Henry Newton – diving full length to deny the midfielder's first-time effort. As the interval beckoned, the Yorkshire side seemed increasingly content with the state of affairs, although they might have had a penalty when Duncan McKenzie went down under a challenge from David Nish.

Leeds reshuffled their formation at half-time with Trevor Cherry replacing Gordon McQueen, who had strained a groin muscle. Harvey continued to be the busier of the goalkeepers, and his save from Bruce Rioch's thunderbolt right-footer was exceptional. Just before the hour mark, Mackay also decided to change his line up, Jeff Bourne replacing Roger Davies who had again struggled to make any real impact. There were two more penalty appeals, which on another occasion could both have been awarded. Cherry seemed to have handled a cross pass from Rioch, and, minutes before the end, Allan Clarke unsuccessfully tried to persuade Mr Richardson that Todd had fouled him. Aside from the penalty claims, the referee booked four players: Frank Gray and Clarke of Leeds and Kevin Hector and Lee of the Rams – although the caution for Lee fell into the category of ridiculous. Having awarded the home side a free-kick just outside the penalty area, the official allowed the Rams striker to fire in a shot which Harvey saved... and then booked him for taking the kick too quickly.

As the teams left the field, thoughts in the press box turned to the possibility of the teams meeting again in the FA Cup seven days later. On the evidence of this display, that contest would be another tight affair, with goals at a premium.

Derby County: Boulton, Thomas, Nish, Rioch, Daniel, Todd, Newton, Gemmill, Davies, Hector, Lee. Substitute: Bourne for Davies (58).

Leeds United: Harvey, Reaney, Gray, Bremner, McQueen, Madeley, McKenzie, Clarke, Lorimer, Yorath, Gray. Substitute: Cherry for McQueen (45).

Attendance: 33,461
Referee: Mr Richardson

Post-match positions: Derby 9, Leeds United 10

Derby v Leeds and tempers rise. Paul Reaney acts as peacemaker between Francis Lee and Leeds goalkeeper David Harvey. In the 1975–76 season Lee became involved with Leeds once more, this time famously with Norman Hunter in a full-scale bout of fisticuffs.

The problem of hooliganism which had plagued many grounds during the season also surfaced at the Leeds game. Police made a number of arrests before the kick-off, and a Derby fan was stabbed as fighting spilled over into the streets surrounding the Baseball Ground after the final whistle. The point dropped saw the Rams slip one place to ninth position, three points behind the leaders Everton, who remained on top despite suffering a 2–1 reversal at Manchester City.

Liverpool grabbed the headlines with a 5–2 demolition of Ipswich Town at Anfield, but then crashed to a surprise 4–1 midweek away defeat against Newcastle United. The Reds never recovered from a three-goal blast from United in the opening 22 minutes, the Magpies' striker Malcolm Macdonald netting two of his side's quartet of strikes. In a month of quiet transfer activity, Tottenham pulled off the most noticeable deal, signing the 21-year-old Bolton Wanderers defender Don McAllister for a fee of £80,000 on 13 February.

With the Rams having already had two matches postponed because of the state of their pitch, a party from the club visited the National Recreation Centre at Crystal Palace on 10 February. The trip was arranged to coincide with the David v Goliath FA Cup replay between Wimbledon and Leeds United at Selhurst Park – a game the First Division side won 1–0. At the centre, the party saw a new nylon-based pitch which, if sanctioned by the Football Association, would cost in excess of £50,000 to install. Although the Rams board subsequently decided that a traditional turf surface remained the best option for them, their minds were again focussed on the ongoing pitch problems when their fifth round tie against Leeds was forced to be rescheduled because the Baseball Ground was yet again rendered unfit by the weather.

Although Mackay remained happy with the strength of his squad, he was required to rearrange his support team when Alan Hill, the Derby youth-team coach, opted to join Brian Clough at Nottingham Forest. Indeed, Hill's move to the City Ground was considered to be something of a coup for Clough – the 31-year-old having earlier left the Nottingham club to rejoin Mackay at the Baseball Ground. In an effort to quickly fill the important vacancy, the Rams boss tried to persuade Theo Foley to relocate to the Midlands from his London base. Foley, the former Charlton Athletic manager, decided against the move, and Ritchie Norman, the ex-Leicester City defender, took on the job before the month concluded. Encouraged by his success in persuading Hill to return, Clough also made an audacious move for Ron Webster. The Rams right-back, having lost his place in the side following his knee injury, was offered terms by Clough after Forest and Derby had agreed a fee of £30,000 for the veteran defender. Webster opted to stay at the Baseball Ground, however, and went on to make another 32 appearances before retiring in 1978. His decision clearly disappointed the Forest manager, who told reporters 'Ron could have done as good a job for us as Dave Mackay did as a player for Derby.' It was a sign of the respect that Clough had for Webster, one of the few senior players to have survived his initial cull of Baseball Ground staff after being appointed as manager.

Undeterred at not being able to persuade Webster to join him, the Forest manager did move into the market before the month concluded. After completing a full assessment of the strength of his squad, he moved quickly to sign a couple of 'old faces.' John McGovern and John O'Hare arrived at Nottingham Forest in a joint fee £60,000 deal from Leeds – less than half the price Clough had paid the Rams for the pair just six months earlier during his managerial spell at the Yorkshire club. With Clough having originally signed McGovern as a 16-year-old at Hartlepools United in 1967, the move represented the fourth time the Scot had agreed to play for his mentor. Amazingly, although McGovern was never rated as one of the game's top performers, he was ultimately to twice lift the European Cup above his head as captain of the Forest team in 1979 and 1980.

STEVE POWELL

18 February 1975
Football Association Cup fifth Round
Derby County 0 v Leeds United 1

Not the way to settle a Cup tie...

Football can be a remarkably cruel game. Anyone doubting that statement should have been at the Baseball Ground for this enthralling rearranged contest, which was sadly decided by an unfortunate own-goal seven minutes from the end. Dave Mackay decided to drop the out-of-form Roger Davies in favour of Jeff Bourne, and with Archie Gemmill suspended, Steve Powell came in for his first start since the game against Queen's Park Rangers on 9 November. Although Gordon McQueen was declared fit to play for the visitors, Jimmy Armfield was forced to name his reserve goalkeeper, David Stewart, his first choice David Harvey having injured his ankle in a car crash three days earlier.

Almost from the outset, this game revolved around the pitting of the Rams' attack against the visitors' defence. In fact, Derby dominated the proceedings to such an extent that Colin Boulton remained a virtual spectator as his teammates tried to unlock the Leeds back four – although on numerous occasions the visitors seemed perfectly happy to make that a back eight. Stewart seemed determined to make the most of his unexpected opportunity, and in the first half he made fine saves – twice from Francis Lee and also from Rod Thomas. As well as looking to be the Rams' best player, Lee also fought a match-long battle with McQueen, Mr Burns adding their names to that of Kevin Hector in his notebook.

After the interval the trend continued with the Rams again surging forward, although their attacks did at times lack the guile that Gemmill brought to the side. Within five minutes of Davies arriving in the 70th minute, Stewart produced his most decisive save – a marvellous catch from an equally impressive overhead kick from Lee. Then, with just seven minutes left, the Rams' dreams of going to Wembley fell apart. Eddie Gray attacked down the left flank and, with his brother Frank overlapping him, was allowed to cross towards the far post. Although the centre evaded the Leeds strikers, David Nish – anticipating a challenge from Duncan McKenzie – attempted to knock the ball away for a corner, but it bounced off his shin and beyond his despairing goalkeeper, the ball no more than trickling into the net. If that was not bad enough, a marvellous chance to equalise was totally wasted. Two minutes later, Bruce Rioch delivered the ball across the six-yard area, only for Davies to prod it wide with the goal gaping in front of him.

Without being overly critical of the visitors, Mackay mused that 'They are the best in the business at coming for a draw, but they're not supposed to win.' His thoughts were clearly with his full-back, who apart from that one touch had, along with Colin Todd, been otherwise magnificent.

Derby County: Boulton, Thomas, Nish, Rioch, Daniel, Todd, Newton, Powell, Bourne, Hector, Lee. Substitute: Davies for Bourne (70).

Leeds United: Stewart, Reaney, Gray, Bremner, McQueen, Madeley, Mckenzie, Clarke, Jordan, Yorath, Gray. Substitute: Hunter.

Attendance: 35,298
Referee: Mr Burns

Post-match positions: n/a

22 February 1975
Football League Division One
Derby County 2 v Arsenal 1

Rams struggle to beat nine-man Gunners...

After the frustration of their FA Cup exit, at least the Rams bounced back to winning ways. The manner of their success, however, was anything but vintage. Arsenal were reduced to 10 men after 15 minutes, and played the last half an hour with just nine. That said, the two points were vital, especially as Liverpool and Everton failed to find the net at Anfield, and fellow title aspirants Ipswich Town were defeated 3–1 at Coventry City.

Dave Mackay opted to play Jeff Bourne at centre-forward, ahead of the out-of-favour Roger Davies. With Steve Powell again replacing the suspended Archie Gemmill in midfield, the manager also gave a rare 12th-man chance to Jeff King. The Gunners, who arrived at the Baseball Ground with nine away defeats to their name, were in the middle of a hectic schedule – their FA Cup fifth round second replay against Leicester City having been arranged for the following Monday evening.

The Rams made a perfect start with David Nish, cast in the role of the unfortunate villain against Leeds, involved in the opening goal. Just two minutes had elapsed when the left-back floated over a corner for Powell to head in at the near post, leaving both Jimmy Rimmer and the line-bound Pat Rice helpless. In an entertaining opening, the visitors forced their way back into the contest almost immediately and won a series of corners. From the third, Kevin Hector broke out of defence only to be kicked at by the already prostrate Alan Ball. Mr Yates decided to caution the Arsenal captain and then, following the midfielder's subsequent complaints, ordered him to the dressing-room. To their credit the Gunners equalised eight minutes later. After Bourne had wasted a good chance, Brian Kidd hit a through pass for John Radford to gallop clear and score. The excitement was maintained when Nish, on his 100th appearance for the club, helped restore the Rams' advantage in the 28th minute. Another corner kick caused problems in the visitors' defence, and when Rimmer fumbled the ball Powell reacted quickly to slot it into the net.

At home, against a team with 10 men, the Rams should have quickly put the game totally beyond Arsenal's reach. Instead they huffed and puffed and made very hard work of claiming the victory – especially after Bob McNab had also been dismissed for dissent in the 61st minute. Of the chances they did create, a Bruce Rioch scorcher hit the post just after the interval and Rimmer saved well from Bourne. At the end the Arsenal manager Bertie Mee shepherded his players away from the referee, clearly not wanting to lose any more of his contingent ahead of the Cup game. For the Rams, although this was not perhaps a particularly attractive fixture, the fact that only 24,000 turned out to watch was again a major disappointment.

Derby County: Boulton, Thomas, Nish, Rioch, Daniel, Todd, Newton, Powell, Bourne, Hector, Lee. Substitute: King.

Arsenal: Rimmer, Rice, McNab, Storey, Mancini, Simpson, Armstrong, Ball, Radford, Kidd, Brady. Substitute: Nelson.

Attendance: 24,002
Referee: Mr Yates
Post-match positions: Derby 7, Arsenal 18

The dismissals at the Baseball Ground marked only the second time since the war that a First Division club had seen two of its players sent off in the same game. On the previous occasion, Arsenal were again involved, Frank McLintock and Peter Storey taking early baths against Burnley at Turf Moor in December 1967. As the Gunners, thanks to a goal from John Radford, overcame Leicester in that second replay, the Rams also turned their thoughts to a midweek fixture – against Ipswich Town at Portman Road. Although Mackay welcomed back Archie Gemmill from suspension, with Steve Powell reverting to the substitutes' bench, it was not a trip that was greeted with any relish. The East Anglian club had won 11 of their 14 home games prior to the Rams' visit, and had conceded just four goals in those fixtures. Sadly Mackay's side could not dent that impressive record. Two first-half strikes put Ipswich firmly in control, and the Rams eventually returned home on the back of a 3–0 scoreline (see report). To compound their frustrations, Francis Lee was forced out of the game with a knee injury, which was to sideline him for several matches. With Everton, thanks to a 3–1 home win against Luton Town, again taking over from Stoke at the top of the table, the Rams slipped to eighth place, the remarkably tight nature of the campaign seeing them thankfully remain just four points behind the Merseysiders. Elsewhere another victory for Leeds, this time against Carlisle United, extended the Yorkshire side's unbeaten sequence to a dozen games. In a third midweek game, Queen's Park Rangers and Middlesbrough shared the points in a 0–0 draw at Loftus Road.

The Gunners' extended tie with Leicester had overshadowed a couple of other notable games in the cup. Fulham created the major surprise of the fifth round, achieving a fine 2–1 victory over Everton at Goodison Park. Meanwhile, in another unexpected result, Peterborough United held Middlesbrough to a 1–1 draw, the Teesiders relying on two goals from Alan Foggon in the replay on 20 February at Ayresome Park to help them gain a berth in the last eight.

25 February 1975
Football League Division One
Ipswich Town 3 v Derby County 0

Derby no match for dominant Ipswich...

The Rams journeyed home from East Anglia after an inept performance allowed the home side to emerge as comfortable winners. More worryingly for Dave Mackay, his entire strike force seemed to have forgotten how to hit the net: the month of February had passed without a recognised forward being on the scoresheet. It was not, however, as if the attackers deserved the full blame for this defeat. Derby gave away two poor goals, the defence, with the exception of Colin Todd, frequently lacking the composure that the return of a fit Roy McFarland would surely have brought.

Encouraged by a Portman Road crowd of 23,078, the home side deservedly went ahead in the 12th minute. A shot from Colin Viljoen was deflected for a corner, the resulting kick being powerfully headed in by David Johnson at the far post. Although the Rams got back into the contest to a degree via their midfield efforts, they created little to worry the Ipswich back four, and in the 42nd minute went 2–0 behind. The lively Johnson, only declared fit before the kick off, again got past Peter Daniel, his centre from the wing being chested down by Mick Lambert for Bryan Hamilton to score with ease; the visitors' defence was left in tatters.

With the Rams' all too infrequent attacks being easily muscled away, it was no surprise when the home side went further ahead in the 68th minute. At least on this occasion the visitors could justifiably point to a dubious refereeing decision. After a corner from the left, Colin Boulton seemed to be impeded – and then again after the ball had come back off the bar. The official saw nothing wrong with the double dose of aggression, however, and, after Kevin Beattie had stabbed the ball in, pointed back to the centre circle. Trailing by three with just 20 minutes remaining, Derby tempers started to fray. Francis Lee was involved in an off-the-ball incident with Hamilton, the challenge making the Rams striker the target of some brutal retribution. In the 87th minute Alan Hunter got in the telling tackle, and Lee limping off gave Steve Powell a very brief appearance.

Along with Todd, only Boulton emerged with any real credit. Although he was beaten three times, he also made significant saves from Johnson and the influential Hamilton. Mackay's summing up told the story. 'Defenders have specific jobs to do,' he told reporters, 'if they don't do them we're in trouble.' The defeat left the Rams with a dozen games to play, their points tally of 34 leaving them needing to win every game to achieve their manager's pre-Christmas demand for a total of at least 56.

Ipswich Town: Sivell, Burley, Mills, Talbot, Hunter, Beattie, Hamilton, Viljoen, Johnson, Whymark, Lambert. Substitute: Woods for Johnson (75).

Derby County: Boulton, Thomas, Nish, Rioch, Daniel, Todd, Newton, Gemmill, Bourne, Hector, Lee. Substitute: Powell for Lee (87).

Attendance: 23,078

Referee: Mr Perkin

Post-match positions: Derby 8, Ipswich 4

Division One – 25 February 1975

		P	W	D	L	GF	GA	PTS
1	Everton	30	12	14	4	44	28	38
2	Stoke City	31	13	11	7	48	36	37
3	Burnley	31	15	7	9	52	45	37
4	Ipswich Town	31	17	2	12	45	29	36
5	Liverpool	30	14	7	9	42	31	35
6	Leeds United	31	14	7	10	43	32	35
7	Manchester City	30	14	7	9	42	41	35
8	**Derby County**	**30**	**13**	**8**	**9**	**44**	**41**	**34**
9	West Ham United	31	11	11	9	48	40	33
10	Middlesbrough	31	11	11	9	38	33	33
11	Queen's Park Rangers	31	12	8	11	41	39	32
12	Newcastle United	30	13	6	11	47	47	32
13	Sheffield United	30	12	8	10	40	42	32
14	Wolverhampton Wdrs	30	10	10	10	39	38	30
15	Coventry City	31	9	12	10	41	47	30
16	Chelsea	30	8	11	11	34	50	27
17	Birmingham City	31	10	6	15	39	48	26
18	Arsenal	29	9	7	13	33	34	25
19	Tottenham Hotspur	32	8	8	16	37	48	24
20	Leicester City	29	6	8	15	27	44	20
21	Luton Town	30	5	10	15	26	43	20
22	Carlisle United	31	8	3	20	30	44	19

CHAPTER EIGHT

March

Hinton returns to spark recovery...

For the first half-hour of this contest the Rams achieved little. They fell behind to an early goal, and were only saved from a home defeat by Alan Hinton – the veteran left-winger who was making his first full appearance since January 1974. Along with Roger Davies, Hinton had been drafted into the side by Dave Mackay after the midweek reversal at Ipswich. With Francis Lee already sidelined for several matches, both men were keen to stake their claims against a Spurs defence shorn of Mike England, the Welsh international who was contemplating his future with the London club.

The visitors took the lead in the 10th minute with a strike netted with a worrying amount of ease. Ralph Coates struck a long pass forward to Chris Jones and, as the Rams defence appealed in vain for offside, the young striker ran on unchallenged to slip the ball past Colin Boulton. It should have been the signal for the home side to shake themselves into action. Instead, they allowed Spurs far too much possession – and if the visitors' finishing had been sharper they would have certainly gone further ahead. With the crowd growing increasingly restless, it was Hinton who set up the equaliser. In the 31st minute he floated over a corner and, although the ball was cleared to the edge of the penalty area, Bruce Rioch volleyed it back beyond everyone and into the net. The power of the shot was such that Pat Jennings, one of the strongest goalkeepers around, could only help the ball on its way. Seven minutes later, Peter Daniel put the Rams in front. Another corner, this time from David Nish, was headed on by Davies for the defender to rush in and nod the ball into the roof of the Spurs net.

Mackay was forced to to adjust his plans just after the interval, when Colin Todd limped off with a knee injury. Steve Powell took over in defence and the Derby rhythm, greatly restored by the goals, was not really disturbed. Although John Duncan had a goal disallowed for offside after his fellow Scot Alfie Conn had hit the bar, the Rams remained the better side and sealed the win in the closing minutes. Hinton, relishing a full game, was again the provider. He delivered a low centre towards Rioch, who knocked the ball back for Davies to blast a first-time left-footer past Jennings. The relief on the marksman's face was clear for all to see, the goal being his first since he scored against Liverpool on 7 December.

Significantly, Davies looked a far better player when he had a regular supply of ammunition from the flanks. No doubt the Rams manager was impressed with the better overall shape the two returnees gave to his side.

Derby County: Boulton, Thomas, Nish, Rioch, Daniel, Todd, Newton, Gemmill, Davies, Hector, Hinton. Substitute: Powell for Todd (50).
Tottenham Hotspur: Jennings, Kinnear, Knowles, McAllister, Pratt, Naylor, Conn, Perryman, Jones, Coates, Duncan. Substitute: Beal.

Attendance: 22,995
Referee: Mr Matthewson
Post-match positions: Derby 7, Tottenham Hotspur 19

The fact that Alan Hinton came back into the line-up so impressively certainly did not surprise Roy McFarland:

'Alan was still full of enthusiasm and loved playing football. He was disappointed every time he wasn't picked in the the team. Alan had great strengths, and could strike a ball any sort of distance with any amount of pace. He would hit the ball, put it into anybody's path. Alan also hit in crosses with pace – as a defender, when you face crosses and they have pace, it doesn't give you much time to get to the ball. Without a doubt, although he was not the best tackler in the world, Alan Hinton had great, great qualities.'

Colin Todd at a glittering night out in London in March. Todd was voted by his fellow professionals the 1975 PFA Player of the Year. Here he accepts his trophy alongside West Ham goalkeeper Mervyn Day (Young Player of the Year) and recently-retired Denis Law, who received a special achievement award for his contribution to football.

Despite the fact that Todd was forced to come off against Tottenham, the nature of his injury did not prevent him from travelling to London 24 hours later to attend the annual awards dinner of the Professional Footballers Association (PFA). Along with Colin Bell, Billy Bonds, Ian Callaghan, Alan Hudson and Duncan McKenzie, the Rams defender had been nominated for the prestigious top award, the 'Footballer of the Year'. It was a journey that proved to be very worthwhile. Todd was announced as the winner and received his trophy from the Prime Minister, Harold Wilson. The decision was a popular one among the professionals in the game, and a clearly delighted Todd acknowledged the significance of the award. 'This is the greatest honour I have ever had, and it's something that will be with me for life. When the other players vote for you, then it really means something.' Before the end of the campaign, Todd was also acknowledged by the Football Writers Association (FWA), who named him as the runner-up in their 'Footballer of the Year' poll. Alan Mullery of Fulham won the award – the Association being swayed by the veteran's contribution to Fulham's impressive form in the FA Cup.

Elsewhere, on the first day of the month, both Everton and Burnley gained significant away victories, results which saw them respectively occupying the top two positions in the table. The Merseysiders won 2–0 against Arsenal, while the Clarets, again inspired by Leighton James, went one better, gaining a 3–0 success at struggling Coventry City. Meanwhile, at Wembley, the all-Second Division League Cup Final between Aston Villa and Norwich City went in favour of the Midlanders, Ray Graydon's 80th-minute penalty follow-up giving Villa the victory.

8 March 1975
Football League Division One
Chelsea 1 v Derby County 2

Impressive Rams stand proud at the Bridge...

Dave Mackay had made his intentions clear before the kick-off to this game. In naming the team the Rams manager selected Jeff Bourne as his substitute in preference to Steve Powell – an extra forward available, if required, to give his team a wider range of attacking possibilities. The typically bold selection was rewarded with a marvellous performance from his side. They dominated the contest from the kick-off and, although Chelsea rallied in the closing stages, anything other than an away victory would have been an injustice.

The visitors knocked the ball around impressively in the first half, and were twice denied only by the woodwork. Alan Hinton, enjoying the spring sunshine in the autumn of his career, saw a shot come back off the post, and John Phillips leaped acrobatically to turn a Peter Daniel header onto the bar. At the other end Colin Boulton – in his 200th League game for the club – was required to make just one save. Ray Wilkins put Ian Britton clear, but the Rams goalkeeper rushed out bravely to smother the ball at the midfielder's feet. Although the Rams were disappointed to go in at half-time still level, their endeavour was rewarded 12 minutes after the restart. Archie Gemmill picked up a loose ball at the edge of his own penalty area, ran forward with pace, and found Roger Davies out on the left. The rejuvenated striker cut in and hit his shot cleverly towards the net, only for Phillips to push the ball up onto the bar. Daniel, who had galloped downfield in support of his captain, read the situation perfectly and managed to knock the rebound into the net. Four minutes later it was 2–0. Kevin Hector was fouled five yards outside of the penalty area, and Hinton drove in a shot which

Victory at the Bridge. Forgotten man Alan Hinton enjoyed a run of eight games when Francis Lee was injured. Derby won six, drew one and lost one during that time, with the veteran having considerable influence. He never started another match for the Rams after this season but here Hinton crashes a free-kick into the Chelsea net to secure a 2–1 win.

flew in after taking a deflection off Steve Finnieston. The wide man enjoyed his celebration and his performance again fully justified his selection.

The visitors' air of satisfaction lasted only a matter of seconds. The veteran Charlie Cooke set off on a mazy dribble before squaring the ball for John Hollins to score with a rasping drive into the net. It was the sign for Chelsea to push ahead in search of the equaliser. The Rams defence held firm though, and although there were a few hectic scrambles around their net, they looked equally dangerous every time they ventured into the Chelsea half of the pitch.

Mackay was delighted with the result, which took his side up to third place. 'Draws are no good for us at this stage of the season. We need to go all out for victory in the rest of our matches if we are to win the Championship' he told Derek Wild of the *Daily Telegraph*.

Chelsea: Phillips, Locke, Sparrow, Hollins, Harris, Hay, Britton, Wilkins, Finnieston, Garland, Cooke. Substitute: Kember.
Derby County: Boulton, Thomas, Nish, Rioch, Daniel, Todd, Newton, Gemmill, Davies, Hector, Hinton. Substitute: Bourne.
Attendance: 22,644
Referee: Mr Briddle
Post-match positions: Derby 3, Chelsea 17

The First Division schedule on 8 March was affected by the games in the sixth round of the FA Cup. Although West Ham United, Fulham and Birmingham City all progressed to the semi-final stage at the expense of Arsenal, Carlisle United and Middlesbrough, the fourth quarter-final contest was only decided after a third replay – a late goal by Clive Woods ultimately giving Ipswich Town a 3–2 win over Leeds United on 27 March.

Todd came through the game at Stamford Bridge unscathed after his minor knee problems, and duly joined up with the rest of the England squad for their international contest against West Germany at Wembley on 12 March, a match Don Revie's side won 2–0. With Rod Thomas also on international duty for Wales, it was a time for Mackay to keep his fingers crossed in the hope that both men would return without any problems and be available for selection against Stoke City. Although the Rams manager was adamant that he would not need to strengthen his team for the run-in, he did complete two minor deals during the early part of the month. Reserve team full-back Alan Lewis joined Brighton for a fee of £9,000, and so linked up again with Peter Taylor, while Mackay also paid Hearts £15,000 for Eric Carruthers – a forward who had impressed reserve-team boss Colin Murphy during a loan spell at the Baseball Ground.

The transfer deadline day on 13 March was a generally subdued affair. Coventry, as sellers, were the busiest team in the First Division. The Sky Blues accepted a bid of £80,000 for Colin Stein from the Scottish side Rangers, and also finally completed the £100,000 deal which took Willie Carr the short distance to Wolverhampton Wanderers, the transfer having fallen through in August 1974 because of the midfielder's injury problems. In the only other major deal, Chris Garland moved from Chelsea to Leicester City, also for £100,000, that deal becoming the 27th in the previous 12 months where a player had moved for a six-figure fee or more. The lack of significant late transfers indicated that, after the surge in activity prior to the season, the majority of clubs were reluctant to spend large amounts in the climate of generally declining attendances.

15 March 1975
Football League Division One
Derby County 1 v Stoke City 2

Greenhoff brace enough to settle Baseball Ground mudbath...

Given the congestion at the top of the First Division, a share of the points at home would have been a poor result for the Rams. To lose them both in the 88th minute with a giveaway goal was an absolute disaster. Indeed, as the crowd of just under 30,000 drifted away from the Baseball Ground, the chances of Derby County emerging as the champions seemed to have evaporated. The fact the game took place at all had surprised many, with Mr Toseland allowing the contest to proceed in a mudbath, which in places squelched over the top of the players' boots.

Such a surface increased the likelihood of mistakes, and in the first half both sides made plenty. That said, although the interval arrived with the contest scoreless, there were significant chances created at either end. For the Potteries team, Ian Moores wasted a pair of opportunities: heading wide when well placed, and then subsequently being foiled by a superb Peter Daniel tackle. Meanwhile, for Derby, Kevin Hector played exceptionally well throughout and seemed to have emerged from his rare barren spell. The Rams striker fired in several efforts in the first half, and was also involved in the move which saw Bruce Rioch chip a shot onto the bar.

Ploughing through the famous Baseball Ground mud are Roger Davies, Henry Newton and Stoke's Dennis Smith. The Rams lost this game and dented their title chances.

The Rams broke the deadlock in the 49th minute, the constantly dangerous Hector being rewarded for his persistence. Archie Gemmill worked a short corner routine with Alan Hinton and, although the cross was cleared, Rod Thomas struck a fierce shot back towards the net. The ball struck a defender and spun to Hector who, played onside by the deflection, slid it past Peter Shilton. Stoke hit back and, with Geoff Hurst on as an additional forward, they equalised in the 75th minute. Geoff Salmons picked up the ball out wide, his centre to the far post being volleyed home by Jimmy Greenhoff, who found himself in acres of space. The Rams defence looked as though they had expected the ball to be delivered in short towards Hurst. It was a terrible goal to concede, but from a defensive standpoint the visitors' winner was even more embarrassing. Thomas clumsily lost out to Dennis Smith, and another Salmons centre was again converted by Greenhoff, this time with a diving header.

Stoke were thus rewarded for their enterprise away from home, with Alan Hudson, alongside Hector and Colin Todd, being one of the few players who truly made light of the atrocious conditions.

Derby County: Boulton, Thomas, Nish, Rioch, Daniel, Todd, Newton, Gemmill, Davies, Hector, Hinton. Substitute: Bourne.

Stoke City: Shilton, Marsh, Lewis, Mahoney, Smith, Dodd, Skeels, Greenhoff, Moores, Hudson, Salmons. Substitute: Hurst for Lewis (61).

Attendance: 29,985

Referee: Mr Toseland

Post-match positions: Derby 6, Stoke City 3

With a sizeable contingent of Stoke fans making the journey up from the Potteries for the game, the spectre of hooliganism again raised its ugly head. As well as there being problems with behaviour before and after the match, fighting also broke out on the Osmaston terrace just before half-time. The incidents led to locals living on the streets around the ground renewing their demands for compensation to be paid for damage to their properties. Their concerns were becoming increasingly common around the country as violence among supporters made the headlines on an all too frequent basis.

There were two remarkable scorelines in other First Division fixtures. Wolverhampton thrashed Chelsea 7–1 at Molineux, and, in a game of even more goals, Ipswich recovered from 3–2 behind to defeat Newcastle United 5–4. In front of 50,084, the largest crowd of the day, Leeds and Everton fought out a scoreless draw at Elland Road. The result left Everton three points clear at the top of the table, with bookmakers assessing them to be odds-on favourites for the title. At the other end of the division, a 3–0 defeat for Tottenham Hotspur at Middlesbrough saw them slip to 20th place, the poor campaign for the London-based teams again emphasised by the fact that alongside Spurs, both Arsenal and Chelsea also remained in the bottom six.

Those odds on the Merseyside club were rapidly adjusted just 72 hours later. To the delight of Mackay, Everton were beaten 2–0 at Middlesbrough, and the Rams manager's sense of happiness further increased the following night when he, along with 3,600 spectators, watched Roy McFarland play 70 minutes of a Central League game against Sheffield United at the Baseball Ground. With Francis Lee also back in full training following his injury sustained against Ipswich, it meant that the Rams would probably have all of their assets available for at least some part of the final four weeks of the campaign.

The other major midweek action centred on Leeds in the European Cup. With the cushion of a 3–0 lead from the first leg of their quarter-final tie against Anderlecht, the Yorkshire side travelled to Brussels for the return game in a confident mood. Their optimism about progressing proved to be well founded, a goal from Billy Bremner giving them an impressive 4–0 aggregate victory, and a pairing against Barcelona in the last four to look ahead to.

---

22 March 1975
Football League Division One
Newcastle United 0 v Derby County 2

Rams maintain challenge with triumph on Tyneside...

Thanks to goals from David Nish and Bruce Rioch, the Rams won at Newcastle for the fourth time in six seasons. They produced another quality performance, this time in the face of a rugged display by the home side – several of the Magpies players committing tackles which were clearly borne out of a frustration at the visitors overall domination. With Everton and Ipswich Town drawing 1–1 at Goodison, the two points gained were vital for Dave Mackay's side – the manager enjoying the post-match celebrations with a large group

DAVID NISH

of his relatives and friends who had travelled down to Tyneside from his native Edinburgh.

Referee Mr Capey, who had a poor game, cautioned Colin Todd after just four minutes, the Rams defender being booked for a deliberate handball offence. It was a great pity, however, that the official did not go on to impose his control throughout the contest. He had already missed several late lunges before another led to the opening goal in the 16th minute. Kevin Hector was felled by the lumbering Glenn Keeley and, although Alan Hinton's free-kick hit the defensive wall, Nish drove in a superb effort which Willie McFaul could only parry onto the underside of the bar. The goalkeeper made a frantic effort to claw the ball back to his body, but the referee's glance at his linesman confirmed that the left-back's shot had already gone over the line. The visitors remained on top, but Newcastle should have equalised before the interval. Colin Boulton flapped at a left-wing corner and was totally out of place as the ball ran loose to Jim Smith. With the goal gaping in front of him, Smith had the time and space to score with ease, but only succeeded in lobbing his effort well over the bar.

In the second half, the Rams had to replace Henry Newton in the 57th minute. After winning a fair tackle with Pat Howard, the midfielder went down in agony after the defender's leg swung through and left him in need of eight stitches in a gash below his knee. It was a brutal attempt to get the ball, and the Newcastle man, returning to the side after a bout of mumps, was very lucky not to be cautioned. The visitors' victory, their sixth away from the Baseball Ground, was sealed three minutes from time with a magnificent goal. From just inside the United half, Rioch ran purposefully towards the net with players reeling in his wake. He had already gone past four would-be tacklers before Keeley was rounded with embarrassing ease – and as McFaul came out to meet him, Rioch coolly struck the ball beyond him and into the net.

It was an excellent solo goal, the Scots 11th in the League and his 16th overall. When asked about the strike, Des Anderson told reporters after the game: 'That's why we paid a lot of money for Bruce.' One thing was certain, however, with goals of such a high quality, £200,000 was starting to look more like a bargain.

Newcastle United: McFaul, Kelly, Hibbitt, Smith, Keeley, Howard, Barrowclough, Nulty, Macdonald, Tudor, Craig. Substitute: Bruce.

Derby County: Boulton, Thomas, Nish, Rioch, Daniel, Todd, Newton, Gemmill, Davies, Hector, Hinton. Substitute: Bourne for Newton (57).

Attendance: 31,010
Referee: Mr Capey

Post-match positions: Derby 7, Newcastle United 13

There was plenty of entertainment in the other First Division fixtures. Stoke defeated Carlisle 5–2 at the Victoria Ground with Geoff Salmons scoring one and setting up the other four of the goals. Meanwhile, in Lancashire, Burnley shared the points with Arsenal, a late penalty by Leighton James giving the Clarets a 3–3 draw. In a third high-scoring fixture, Sheffield United – thanks to a marvellous display by Tony Currie – recovered from a 2–1 half-time deficit to beat West Ham 3–2. The important game at Goodison Park between title contenders Everton and Ipswich ended in a 1–1 draw which, given the Rams' away victory, allowed the Rams manager to enjoy his Saturday night even more.

It all meant that the Rams could look forward to their three-game Easter programme with anticipation, especially as their fixtures against Luton Town and Manchester City were at the Baseball Ground. The middle fixture of the trio looked on paper to be potentially the hardest to win. Burnley had been unbeaten at home in the League for 13 matches, and were a side capable of scoring plenty of goals. The Clarets also stood one place above the Rams in the table, with the pre-Easter standings for the top 10 teams reading as follows:

Division One – 22 March 1975

		P	W	D	L	GF	GA	PTS
1	Everton	35	14	16	5	49	32	44
2	Ipswich Town	35	19	3	13	53	36	41
3	Middlesbrough	35	15	11	9	47	34	41
4	Liverpool	35	15	11	9	48	35	41
5	Stoke City	35	15	11	9	56	43	41
6	Burnley	35	16	9	10	60	51	41
7	**Derby County**	**34**	**16**	**8**	**10**	**52**	**45**	**40**
8	Sheffield United	34	15	9	10	45	44	39
9	Queen's Park Rangers	36	15	8	13	48	36	38
10	Manchester City	35	15	8	12	46	48	38

29 March 1975
Football League Division One
Derby County 5 v Luton Town 0

All five for Davies... and he could have scored more...

There was just one change to the Rams team that faced Luton Town at the Baseball Ground, with Powell coming in for the injured Newton. Roger Davies enjoyed his finest hour in a Derby County shirt as the Rams demolished Luton. He scored all five goals, and in so doing became the first Derby player since Hughie Gallacher to achieve that feat. The fact that Gallacher netted his five against Newcastle United as far back as the 1934–35 season merely emphasised what an impressive individual performance it was. Remarkably, such was the Rams' domination that it could have been more. The striker had another two efforts disallowed, and had they counted he would have tallied five in the first half alone.

The rout started as early as the ninth minute. After pressing forward, the home side won a corner and Davies rose above the

It was Roger Davies's day on 29 March as the lanky forward bagged all five against Luton Town as the Rams' drive for the title gathered momentum. The first saw Big Rog leap to head in a Hinton cross with Peter Daniel looking on. Future Ram Paul Futcher is the Luton defender to the left.

'Nice One Roger, Let's Have Another One' was the cry from the Pop Side and Luton keeper Keith Barber is well beaten by this header from a Rod Thomas centre.

Davies was a constant threat to the Hatters. Here he chips the ball goalwards again.

Roger might have had seven if two efforts had not been disallowed. This diving header was ruled offside by referee Tinkler. Gemmill is partly hidden behind the Luton defender, Steve Buckley, who would go on to play 366 times for the Rams, as a fine servant of the club between 1978 and 1986. Derby could have signed him for next to nothing if they had spotted him playing locally for Ilkeston Town or Burton Albion, although even at £163,000 from Luton he represented Tommy Docherty's best signing for the Rams.

The architect from the wing... Alan Hinton, who was the provider of a couple of Roger Davies's five goals against the Hatters.

defence to head in Alan Hinton's precise centre. Four minutes later, a move down the right allowed Rod Thomas to loft the ball into the penalty area. Although the cross was slightly overhit, Davies again timed his jump perfectly – his header going in despite the frantic efforts of the Hatters' full-back John Ryan to keep it out. Netting two early goals certainly filled the Rams striker with confidence and, in open play, he began to avoid his marker John Faulkner with some comfort. The hat-trick strike arrived just after the half hour with Thomas, relishing the chance to get forward, again involved. He delivered a long pass which split open the visitors' rearguard, and Davies ran on to smash a shot past Paul Barber, who remained rooted to his line. Before the interval, the beleaguered Luton goalkeeper saw Davies beat him twice more. Archie Gemmill nodded the ball back to the striker, who netted the chance just as Mr Tinkler blew for offside. Then, after a marvellous pass from Hinton had set him free, Davies unfortunately controlled the ball with his hand before placing yet another effort beyond the goalkeeper.

Although the Rams' control of the match resumed unabated after the break, it was not until the final stages that Davies struck again. In the 78th minute, he latched on to a weak back header from Ryan and, with Barber out of place, cracked the ball beyond him and into the net. The massacre was completed eight minutes later when another astute Hinton pass eluded Faulkner and Davies scored with a well-taken shot. As the ball went in, he turned away in celebration, his face a picture of sheer disbelief at what he had achieved.

Before the final whistle, Kevin Hector tried to set up a sixth goal for Davies, but Barber denied him with a great save at the expense of a corner. At the end, the hero of the day went off to a splendid reception, the Luton players sportingly adding their own congratulations to the lanky striker. All in all, it was a day not to be forgotten.

Derby County: Boulton, Thomas, Nish, Rioch, Daniel, Todd, Powell, Gemmill, Davies, Hector, Hinton. Substitute: Bourne.

Luton Town: Barber, Ryan, Buckley, Anderson, Faulkner, Futcher, Ryan, Husband, Futcher, West, Aston. Substitute: Seasman for Husband (72).

Attendance: 24,169

Referee: Mr Tinkler

Post-match positions: Derby 6, Luton Town 21

---

31 March 1975
Football League Division One
Burnley 2 v Derby County 5

Brilliant Rams score five more...

Derby County scored five goals away from home in a League game for the first time since Kevin Hector destroyed Cardiff City in September 1967. Some 324 League games later, the ultra-resilient Hector was again on the scoresheet as the Rams disposed of Burnley with a ruthless exhibition of attacking football. Ten goals in two games was certainly an impressive feat. As well as doing wonders for the Rams' goal average, it also meant that all of the other clubs with title aspirations were made aware that Derby had rapidly become the team that they needed to finish ahead of.

HENRY NEWTON

Confidence surged through Dave Mackay's side from the kick-off, and they took the lead in the first minute. Bruce Rioch intercepted a dreadful pass from Billy Ingham and rounded James Thomson before slipping the ball past a bemused Alan Stevenson. Such a start at least jolted the Clarets into action. For a short time they competed well, with their left-winger Leighton James looking an obvious danger. Indeed it was the Welsh international who set up the equaliser in the 18th minute. He floated over a corner towards the powerful Ray Hankin who planted a firm header into the net – despite Colin Boulton's claim that he had been impeded in trying to reach the ball.

The celebrations on the Turf Moor terracing were short-lived, however. Just two minutes later, Alan Hinton was felled by a retreating Keith Newton three yards outside the penalty area. As the Rams man shaped to take the free-kick himself, David Nish ran up and curled a magnificent strike over the defensive wall and beyond the goalkeeper. It was a stunning goal – and so well taken that Stevenson never even moved as the ball flashed by him. In the 29th minute Derby went 3–1 in front. Colin Todd knocked out a pass to Hector, who quickly turned in a low cross which Roger Davies flicked home at the far post. Trailing at home, Burnley had no option but to try and claw themselves back into the game. Although Boulton made a brilliant save from a Derrick Parker header after the interval, he had no chance with the Clarets' second goal in the 75th minute. Peter Noble got clear and was upended by Peter Daniel. It was an obvious penalty, and James hit the spot-kick beyond the goalkeeper's left hand.

Again the Rams responded instantly. Hinton fired in a volley that was too hot for Stevenson to hold, and Hector, reacting faster than anyone else, squeezed the ball home. In the final moments Hector completed his brace, turning in a low cross from Hinton with the Burnley defence again spreadeagled.

Jack Taylor refereed the contest poorly. The World Cup final official was pursued 50 yards by Boulton after allowing the first

Burnley goal, and later cautioned Daniel for apparently displaying 'an aggressive attitude.' With Manchester City completing the Rams' trio of Easter fixtures, a Baseball Ground victory would move Mackay's side even closer to their dream. At the ideal time, Derby County were undoubtably the First Division's 'in form' team.

Burnley: Stevenson, Newton, Brennan, Noble, Waldron, Thomson, Flynn, Ingham, Hankin, Parker, James. Substitute: Rodaway.

Derby County: Boulton, Thomas, Nish, Rioch, Daniel, Todd, Powell, Gemmill, Davies, Hector, Hinton. Substitute: Bourne.

Attendance: 24,276

Referee: Mr Taylor

Post-match positions: Derby 5, Burnley 7

Division One – 31 March 1975

		P	W	D	L	GF	GA	PTS
1	Everton	37	15	16	6	50	35	46
2	Liverpool	38	17	11	10	53	37	45
3	Stoke City	38	16	13	9	61	46	45
4	Ipswich Town	37	20	4	13	55	37	44
5	**Derby County**	**36**	**18**	**8**	**10**	**62**	**47**	**44**
6	Middlesbrough	37	16	11	10	50	36	43
7	Burnley	37	16	9	12	62	58	41
8	Sheffield United	36	15	10	11	47	47	40
9	Manchester City	37	16	8	13	48	50	40
10	Leeds United	36	14	11	11	49	39	39
11	Queen's Park Rangers	38	15	9	14	50	49	39
12	West Ham United	37	12	13	12	55	49	37
13	Wolverhampton Wdrs	37	13	10	14	54	49	36
14	Newcastle United	37	14	8	15	55	64	36
15	Birmingham City	37	13	8	16	48	52	34
16	Coventry City	37	10	14	13	48	57	34
17	Arsenal	36	11	10	15	42	43	32
18	Chelsea	37	9	13	15	40	64	31
19	Leicester City	36	9	11	16	38	53	29
20	Tottenham Hotspur	37	10	8	19	42	56	28
21	Luton Town	37	8	10	19	36	60	26
22	Carlisle United	37	10	3	24	38	55	23

CHAPTER NINE
April

1 April 1975
Football League Division One
Derby County 2 v Manchester City 1

Rioch gives Derby Easter maximum...

Although Bruce Rioch once again grabbed the headlines for his goalscoring prowess, this victory was based on a courageous overall team performance. The strain of playing three games in four days understandably took its toll on the energy-sapping Baseball Ground surface, and at times towards the end an old-fashioned hoof to safety was as good as the Rams could manage. That said, their flowing attacks in the first hour produced two marvellous goals, and eventually produced the result which moved them up into joint first place in the table alongside Ipswich Town and Everton.

Joe Corrigan was the busier goalkeeper in the opening minutes, and saved efforts from both Kevin Hector and Roger Davies in quick succession. However, in the 27th minute, the inspirational Archie Gemmill went past Colin Bell by the corner flag, and his cross was headed against the post by Davies – with the City shot-stopper for once well beaten. With the interval beckoning, Rioch finally opened the scoring. David Nish, who looked menacing every time he ventured up the flank, passed neatly to Hector who went wide and centred for Rioch to strike with a rare full-length diving header. Within six minutes of the restart it was 2–0. Davies dribbled past Tommy Booth and, after realising his options were limited, laid the ball back perfectly into Rioch's path. As usual, the midfielder did not need to be encouraged to pull the trigger, his left-foot 25-yard drive leaving Corrigan helpless by his right-hand post.

As the Rams tired, Steve Powell for example battling on with a thigh injury, the balance of power changed and City came back into the game. With Bell leading their revival, Rod Thomas did remarkably well to halt the midfielder at the expense of a corner – and then to kick the resulting set piece to safety after Rodney Marsh had conjured up an acrobatic overhead kick. It was in fact Bell who gave the Mancunians a glimmer of hope seven minutes from the end. He collected a pass from Marsh and delivered a firm shot past Colin Boulton from a dozen yards out.

In the electric atmosphere, tempers flared at regular intervals throughout the contest. Mr Kew booked Rioch, Davies and Gemmill for Derby and Asa Hartford for the visitors. Incredibly, however, he failed to caution Marsh for any of his 'tackles' – the majority of which were sky high with studs clearly visible. At times the City striker seemed to frustrate even his most loyal of followers, his undoubted ability being overtaken by moments of temper which resulted in potentially brutally dangerous challenges.*

Derby County: Boulton, Thomas, Nish, Rioch, Daniel, Todd, Powell, Gemmill, Davies, Hector, Hinton. Substitute: Lee.

Manchester City: Corrigan, Hammond, Donachie, Doyle, Booth, Oakes, Hartford, Bell, Marsh, Tueart. Substitute: Barnes.

Attendance: 32,996

Referee: Mr Kew

Post-match positions: Derby 3, Manchester City 10

*Note: By January 1976, Rodney Marsh had deserted the British game for a chance to play in the North American Soccer League, football in the United States having been revitalised by the arrival of Pelé at the New York Cosmos the previous summer. His apparent disillusionment with England was summed up on departure by the following quote – 'Football here is a grey game, played on grey days, by grey people.'

Although Ipswich Town moved to the top of the table on goal average with a 3–2 victory against Birmingham City, six Easter points out of six was a magnificent haul for the Rams. Indeed it prompted Dave Mackay to comment 'I have been saying all along that we can win the championship, and we have put the results together at the right time. Everton are perhaps now our biggest threat, but I feel that our remaining games are a bit easier than those of the rest of other challengers.' His comment regarding the outstanding games was a valid one. A glance at the table and fixtures left to play read as follows:

Division One – 1 April 1975

		P	W	D	L	GF	GA	PTS
1	Ipswich Town	38	21	4	13	58	39	46
2	Everton	37	15	16	6	50	35	46
3	**Derby County**	**37**	**19**	**8**	**10**	**64**	**48**	**46**
4	Liverpool	38	17	11	10	53	37	45
5	Stoke City	38	16	13	9	61	46	45
6	Middlesbrough	37	16	11	10	50	36	43
7	Burnley	38	16	9	13	64	62	41
8	Sheffield United	37	15	11	11	48	48	41
9	Leeds United	37	14	12	11	50	40	40
10	Manchester City	38	16	8	14	49	52	40

	Home	*Away*
Ipswich T	Queens Park R West Ham U	Manchester C Leeds U
Everton	Burnley Sheffield U	Luton T Newcastle U Chelsea
Derby C	**Wolverhampton W West Ham U Carlisle U**	**Middlesbrough Leicester C**
Liverpool	Carlisle U Queens Park R	Leeds U Middlesbrough
Stoke C	Chelsea Newcastle U	Sheffield U Burnley
Middlesbrough	Derby C Liverpool	Leicester C Wolverhampton W Coventry C
Burnley	Tottenham H Stoke C	Everton Manchester C

Kevin Hector shields the ball from Manchester City's Willie Donachie during the vital 2–1 Baseball Ground win on 1 April. Bruce Rioch hit both the Derby goals as the attendance finally crept up to around the 33,000 mark, the public at last realising they had a team to watch that could entertain and lift the Championship trophy.

5 April 1975
Football League Division One
Middlesbrough 1 v Derby County 1

Last-gasp Hector grabs vital point...

After creating nothing for 89 minutes, the Rams were gifted a goal that gave them a share of the spoils at a wintry Ayresome Park. Although Jack Charlton was left in a rage, Dave Mackay departed for home probably believing that, given their luck in getting the point, Derby County's name was close to being engraved on the Championship trophy. With three of their remaining four fixtures at the Baseball Ground, the Rams ultimate destiny remained their own to decide – Mackay's only worry being a groin injury to David Nish which saw the defender limp off after just a quarter of an hour.

With the inclement conditions making the surface increasingly difficult, this was never going to be a classic encounter. The home side had the best of the early exchanges, with Bobby Murdoch, their ex-Celtic midfielder, being behind almost everything of note that they created. Opposing him stride for stride and trick for trick, however, was Archie Gemmill, who, after an uncertain start to his captaincy, had led the Rams magnificently throughout the campaign. Although neither goalkeeper was called upon to make a worthwhile save in the opening 30 minutes, the opening goal five minutes later was worth the wait. Murdoch hit an astute 30-yard pass in the direction of David Armstrong, who managed to get his foot to the ball as Colin Boulton advanced towards him. The diversion from Armstrong ran across the goal area and David Mills just eluded the retreating Peter Daniel to run home the ball at the far post.

After the interval, the visitors played with more purpose, and yet it was still the Teesiders who had the best of the chances, Murdoch and Armstrong both firing high and wide from good positions. With time running out, Alan Foggon should have put the contest well beyond the Rams' grasp. The burly striker dispossessed Henry Newton and raced clear with only Boulton to beat. It was a golden opportunity, but Foggon hesitated, and although he managed a shot, the goalkeeper dived to his left to parry the ball and then clutch it to his body. Even though the score remained at 1–0, there seemed little danger ahead of Stuart Boam when he took possession deep in his own half in the final minute. However, instead of clearing the ball downfield, the defender only managed to give it to Roger Davies – who in turn slipped it to Kevin Hector. In a flash Hector had shaken off Willie Maddren and fired home a marvellous shot which went past Jim Platt and in at the far post.

A delighted Rams chairman, Sam Longson, acknowledged his side for their persistence. 'With a capital P,' he told Gerald Mortimer of the *Derby Evening Telegraph*. Charlton's attitude, meanwhile, could not have been more of a contrast. 'They threw away a season's work with one result,' was the gist of what the Middlesbrough manager had to say, the expletives from his comments being removed for those of a sensitive disposition.

Middlesbrough: Platt, Craggs, Cooper, Souness, Boam, Maddren, Murdoch, Mills, Hickton, Foggon, Armstrong. Substitute: Brine for Hickton (80).

Derby County: Boulton, Thomas, Nish, Rioch, Daniel, Todd, Newton, Gemmill, Davies, Hector, Hinton. Substitute: Bourne for Nish (15).

Attendance: 30,066

Referee: Mr Grey

Post-match positions: Derby 4, Middlesbrough 6

With Nish ruled out of the Rams' midweek game, Mackay seized the chance to bring Roy McFarland back into the first team, the centre-half having come through a series of reserve-team fixtures without a problem. Thirty years later the England centre-half recalled his thoughts at returning after such a long absence: 'I was certainly a little bit apprehensive. I had seen the majority of the games, but it had been very frustrating sitting in the stands watching what was going off.' Although the game against Wolverhampton was far from a classic (see report), given the defeat of Everton at Luton Town, Francis Lee's goal was almost priceless as it took the Rams clear at the top of the table for the first time in the campaign.

Elsewhere, Leeds United achieved a 2–1 win against Barcelona in the first leg of their European Cup semi-final, goals from Billy Bremner and Allan Clarke giving Jimmy Armfield's side the slight advantage ahead of the return leg in Spain. Domestically, the FA Cup semi-finals were decided after replays. West Ham United, thanks to a brace from Alan Taylor, beat Ipswich 2–1 at Maine Road, and at Stamford Bridge a single strike by John Mitchell enabled Fulham to defeat Birmingham.

---

9 April 1975
Football League Division One
Derby County 1 v Wolverhampton W 0

Lee strike decisive as McFarland boosts Rams...

After an 11-month absence, Roy McFarland returned to the Rams side as they defeated the visitors by a single goal. The England centre-half had a magnificent game, his performance being described by Dave Mackay as 'out of this world.' Just as had been the case at Middlesbrough, this was not a great contest, but with middle-of-the-table Wolves seemingly determined to defend from the outset, at least this time the Rams created a significant number of chances.

To a great reception, McFarland was announced in the number three shirt to replace David Nish, Francis Lee also returning to the

One of the most poignant moments of a great season. It is 9 April 1975 and heady days of spring for Derby County, on the verge of a second League Championship. Roy McFarland had missed the majority of the season with his Achilles tendon injury. For Wolves' visit McFarland returned and Daniel moved to left-back, but retained the number five shirt he had worn so well all season. After the 1–0 win Roy Mac leaves the field and here we see Daniel waiting to shake him by the hand.

line-up in place of Alan Hinton, who reverted to the substitutes' bench. While McFarland immediately took up a central position, Peter Daniel, his deputy for so long, played splendidly at left-back and demonstrated what versatility he offered the club in his 11th season as a Baseball Ground professional.

In the first period, the Rams' finishing could have been better. Although Bruce Rioch smashed a shot against the goalkeeper's chest, Kevin Hector, Daniel and McFarland all missed good chances to put their side ahead. After the break the trend continued: Francis Lee saw a marvellous effort knocked away by Gary Pierce, and several other opportunities either hit a defender and bounced to safety, or just missed the target.

The crucial goal came in the 69th minute. Archie Gemmill curled over an inswinging corner and Mike Bailey only succeeded in heading the ball towards his own net. Despite the fact that there was a defender covering the line, Lee nipped in and touched the ball home from close range. It was the slightest of deflections, but the Rams striker wheeled away in triumph, certainly in no doubt whatsoever that he had notched his 16th strike of the campaign.

As Wolves started to look a well-beaten team, Kenny Hibbert marred an otherwise excellent display by being cautioned for dissent in the 80th minute. Indeed, with Lee looking as though he wanted to quickly make up for his spell on the sidelines, the Rams could have added to their advantage.

The importance of the win was magnified enormously within minutes of the final whistle, news coming through from Kenilworth Road that Everton had slipped to a 2–1 defeat against Luton Town. With Saturday home games against West Ham United and Carlisle United remaining, the turnstiles would be closed before kick-off at both matches. However, despite the Rams' attacking policy throughout the season, only a handful more than 30,000 watched this victory – a terribly poor figure given the irresistibly competitive nature of the First Division.

Derby County: Boulton, Thomas, McFarland, Rioch, Daniel, Todd, Newton, Gemmill, Davies, Hector, Lee. Substitute: Hinton.

Wolverhampton Wanderers: Pierce, Palmer, Parkin, Bailey, Jefferson, McAlle, Hibbitt, Carr, Withe, Farley, Daley. Substitute: Gardner for Farley (78).

Attendance: 30,109
Referee: Mr Bent
Post-match positions: Derby 1, Wolverhampton Wanderers 13

12 April 1975
Football League Division One
Derby County 1 v West Ham United 0

Hinton's arrival sets Rams on path to victory...

The Rams achieved another single-goal success, this time against a West Ham side which seemed to have already turned its thoughts to the FA Cup final at Wembley on 3 May. Although Dave Mackay decided to name the same forward line that had played against Wolverhampton Wanderers, it was not until he introduced Alan Hinton to the fray that the contest was decided. With David Nish also passed fit to play, the home team took to the field with an all-international back four – the pick of whom was Rod Thomas, who had a magnificent contest and totally snuffed out the rare attacks that the Hammers managed to create.

West Ham, as always, were neat in their approach play, although it was the home side who had the best of the opportunities in the first half. On another occasion, perhaps when the tension was less, the half chances they created would have been converted. With Roger Davies, playing despite a stomach upset, being particularly unlucky, the Rams again saw their efforts either blocked by flying defenders or going just wide of the post. In the 63rd minute Mackay, who had utilised his substitutes so well in earlier games, again opted to change his formation. The arrival of Hinton in place of the under-

Archie Gemmill burst past the West Ham United defence of John McDowell, Alan Taylor and Billy Bonds as the Rams recorded a 1-0 victory with another goal from Bruce Rioch.

standably tiring Davies immediately gave the attack a greater potency – the winger utilising his ability to go past defenders at pace from the outset. The veteran, who had enjoyed a marvellously successful cameo role in the run-in to the Championship finale, again came up with a hand in the breakthrough. In the 66th minute, he delivered a corner to the far post and, although the ball bobbled around, Bruce Rioch struck a low shot through a crowd of players and decisively past Mervyn Day. As well as breaking the deadlock, the goal also noticeably eased the nervousness of the Baseball Ground crowd of just over 31,000. Derby were transformed by the goal and, inspired by Hinton, they went in search of a second. Nish just failed to get a touch to a clever Kevin Hector centre across the six-yard area, and Francis Lee hit the post after a cunning left-flank delivery from the substitute had left Day well out of position.

The victory extended the Rams' late-season surge – and took their points tally for the last seven games to 13, the draw at Middlesbrough being the only blot on an otherwise winning sequence. Significantly, their defence also looked tighter with McFarland back in action. With just two games remaining, the champagne went on ice and supporters left the ground getting ready to celebrate a second Championship in four seasons.

Derby County: Boulton, Thomas, Nish, Rioch, McFarland, Todd, Newton, Gemmill, Davies, Hector, Lee. Substitute: Hinton for Davies (63).

West Ham United: Day, McDowell, Lampard, Bonds, Taylor, Lock, Jennings, Paddon, Taylor, Brooking, Gould. Substitute: Holland for Taylor (70).

Attendance: 31,536
Referee: Mr Lowe

Post-match positions: Derby 1, West Ham 13

---

19 April 1975
Football League Division One
Leicester City 0 v Derby County 0

Solid point for Rams as title draws nearer...

On the day that the season-long congestion at the top of the First Division eventually started to ease, the Rams gained another vital point from their visit to Filbert Street. Any doubts that their scoreless draw represented a point lost rather than one won were quickly dispelled by news of the other results. Back in their dressing room, the Rams learned that both of the Merseyside challengers for the title had been defeated: Liverpool slipping to a 1–0 reversal at Middlesbrough and, more importantly, Everton, after going 2–0 ahead, crashing to a 3–2 home defeat against Sheffield United.

Encouraged by the sight of thousands of visiting supporters packing the terraces (indeed, hundreds of Derby supporters were locked out of the full house), the Rams attacked from the kick-off. As they swept forward, only the impressive Mark Wallington prevented them from going ahead. After Roger Davies had been sent clear by a superb Archie Gemmill pass, the man given the task of replacing Peter Shilton forced the Rams striker wide and recovered well to divert the subsequent shot for a corner. When Bruce Rioch

ALAN HINTON

also went close with a thundering shot which just went the wrong side of the post, it seemed to be only a matter of time before the breakthrough came. However, Leicester, who themselves were fighting relegation, and needed a point to ensure their safety, rallied with a couple of smart moves. The mercurial Frank Worthington stabbed a shot just wide, and Colin Boulton timed his leap perfectly to clutch on to an inviting cross from Chris Garland. These were signs for the visitors to reduce their attacking tendencies, and instead rely a little more on the coolness and experience of their back four to extinguish any ongoing threat that City might pose.

In fact, as the contest proceeded after the interval, both defensive quartets became more dominant and few additional chances were created. Dave Mackay for once resisted the urge to go for the victory, and although Alan Hinton warmed up, he was not called into action. Just before the final whistle, Davies did get clear but, after confidently going past two defenders, his dangerous centre was knocked to safety by John Sammels. When the referee did blow for time, the Leicester manager Jimmy Armfield shared his relief at staying up with the Rams, the champagne he delivered to them being consumed as the other scorelines crackled through on the radio.

As a consequence of the day's events, only Ipswich Town were left with a chance of overtaking Mackay's side. For the East Anglian side to win the championship the Rams would need to be defeated by Carlisle United, and Bobby Robson's men would need maximum points from their fixtures against Manchester City and West Ham United.

Leicester City: Wallington, Whitworth, Rofe, Lee, Blockley, Cross, Weller, Sammels, Worthington, Birchenall, Garland. Substitute: Stringfellow for Garland (86).

Derby County: Boulton, Thomas, Nish, Rioch, McFarland, Todd, Newton, Gemmill, Davies, Hector, Lee. Substitute: Hinton.

Attendance: 38,493

Referee: Mr Reynolds

Post-match positions: Derby 1, Leicester City 16

Relegated Carlisle United visited the Baseball Ground for the last game of the season. Shafestbury Street was suitably adorned and fans began arriving hours before kick-off at the Baseball Ground. Note the 60p admission charge on turnstile

24. Derby won both their League Championships in the white and blue strip (with red numbers!). They changed from black to blue shorts in 1970 and reverted back to the black in the late 1980s.

Ahead of their final League fixture, the Rams entertained Stoke City on 22 April in a testimonial game for Colin Boulton. Although the home side won by a convincing 4–1 scoreline, the crowd of just 7,767 was a disappointment given that the recipient had been at the Baseball Ground for over a decade and had just set a new appearance record for goalkeepers. However, any frustrations that the organisers felt at the lack of interest in the game were dispelled the following night when Ipswich failed to win at Maine Road – the result that confirmed the Rams as the champions. Remarkably, just as had been the case in 1972, the Derby players heard news of their success while together as a group. Under Brian Clough's management the squad had celebrated in Cala Millor. Second time around the location was at least a little closer, Bailey's nightclub in Derby city centre, where the team had gathered for their end-of-season awards ceremony.

The champagne flowed late into the night, with the biggest cheer of the evening, apart from that which greeted the news from Manchester at around 9.10pm, being reserved for Peter Daniel. The supporters' club chose him as their 'Player of the Year,' the modest defender describing the award as 'the proudest moment of my career.' With Francis Lee already having a Championship medal from his career with Manchester City, he joined the exclusive band of players who had won the title with two different clubs. He revealed that the sense of achievement was as strong as ever. 'Of course this means just as much as my medals with Manchester City. It has been a magnificent effort, and we have only really felt any pressure in the last four games.'

While the players relaxed ahead of their final fixture, the Rams' administration staff went into overdrive. Their pre-match planning for the Carlisle United game was finalised to perfection, with the parade of former players on the day proving to be a marvellously emotional memory for all those who witnessed it. Derby County were the champions, and the fact was celebrated in style, at least until three o'clock when Mr Morrissey blew his whistle.

26 April 1975
Football League Division One
Derby County 0 v Carlisle United 0

Mood of celebration extends into last game...

The Rams were presented with the League Championship Trophy by Sam Bolton, a vice-president of the Football League, prior to the kick-off. It came after a superbly organised parade of former players, all of whom were enthusiastically greeted by the capacity crowd. Perhaps it was the nostalgia of the occasion, or more likely the relief at overcoming the tension of the final weeks of the season – whatever, Dave Mackay's side relaxed into the party atmosphere, and what followed the pre-match festivities was as poor a contest as the Baseball Ground had witnessed for some time. Thankfully, it did not matter and Mackay was able to reflect: 'Ok, after all that fun, I

The club acted swiftly following Ipswich's failure to win on the previous Wednesday and arranged a parade of former heroes before the kick-off. Behind them, on a sweltering Pop Side, the style of the era was for banners and scarves and the banners on the Ley Stand swagger with a touch of arrogance – 'We Are the Champions – Again!' That is how big a club the Rams really were in those halcyon days of the mid 1970s.

Proud manager Dave Mackay and assistant Des Anderson lead out the champions.

Mackay and Anderson with the League Championship trophy.

am afraid we turned it off when we should have turned it on. Still I'm not going to complain after such as magnificent season.' In contrast to the Rams' mood Carlisle, who formed a guard of honour as Derby walked out, were playing their last First Division game for other reasons – the Cumbrians had already been relegated after just one campaign in the top flight.

In the first half, Archie Gemmill had the best chance to open the scoring, but the Rams captain shot wide after being sent clear by Bruce Rioch. Although the visitors' goalkeeper Alan Ross was required to save from Colin Todd and Roger Davies, far too many of the Rams' passes went astray, and again only the arrival of Alan Hinton after 58 minutes threatened to lift the game from its mediocrity. The left-winger delivered a series of crosses, which at least increased the pressure on the visitors' defence. From one such centre, Ross was injured as Kevin Hector challenged him, but he recovered well and before the final whistle made excellent stops from a Hinton thunderbolt and a clever header from Hector.

To their credit, at least Carlisle created a few chances of their

Colin Todd lifts aloft the *Daily Express* Sports Writers Footballer of the Year trophy, another richly-deserved accolade for this most talented of defenders.

own. Their football had often been neat throughout the campaign, but they had, as was the case here, often lacked decisiveness in front of the net. John Laidlaw did force Colin Boulton into making a couple of routine saves, but generally they lacked the guile to disturb the Rams defence, within which the excellent Roy McFarland completed his fourth comeback game after his long absence.

The scenes at the end were remarkable as fans took to the pitch to enjoy their moment of triumph. With regard to the infamous surface, the Rams directors had earlier announced plans to lay a new one costing in excess of £40,000 – the club having already offered, with in excess of 1,000 takers, pieces of the old turf at £2 each as a memento of the Championship season.

Derby County: Boulton, Thomas, Nish, Rioch, McFarland, Todd, Newton, Gemmill, Davies, Hector, Lee. Substitute: Hinton for Lee (58).

Carlisle United: Ross, Carr, Spearritt, O'Neil, Green, Parker, Martin, Train, Clarke, Laidlaw, Balderstone. Substitute: Owen.

Attendance: 36,882

Referee: Mr Morrissey

Post-match positions: Derby 1, Carlisle United 22

Roger Davies.

Derby County: Champions 1974-75

Francis Lee added a second Championship medal
to the one he won at Manchester City in
1967–68. Roy McFarland had won one in
1971–72 with Derby and came back from his
injury in the last four games of 1974–75 (all
clean sheets) to share in the Rams' latest glory.

Derby County: Champions 1974-75

Bring on the Champions! This picture was not rehearsed. With the trophy, on the mudbath, from left to right, back row: Des Anderson, Dave Mackay, Roger Davies, Henry Newton, Colin Boulton, Roy McFarland, Alan Hinton,

Francis Lee, Jeff Bourne (hidden), David Nish, Peter Daniel, Colin Todd, Steve Powell. Front row: Rod Thomas, Bruce Rioch, Archie Gemmill and Kevin Hector. A squad of 16 players had won the League Championship.

David Nish and Kevin Hector parade the trophy past the Normanton End goal, with goalkeeper Colin Boulton, unique in being ever-present in both Rams Championship-winning seasons, trotting behind.

With the Rams confirmed as champions, the other fixtures on 26 April helped finalise the qualification places for the UEFA Cup and also the three relegation places. Liverpool confirmed their position as runners-up with a 3–1 home victory against Queen's Park Rangers, while Ipswich finished third after their last game 4–1 success over West Ham. Both second and third-placed teams entered the European competition, alongside Everton who had grabbed fourth place ahead of Stoke. At the other end of the table, Carlisle had already been relegated before their visit to the Baseball Ground, and they were joined by Chelsea, who could only manage a 1–1 draw at Stamford Bridge against Everton. The final relegation berth was decided 48 hours later when, as a consequence of Tottenham Hotspur defeating Leeds, Luton Town's one-season stay in the top flight also came to an end. For the 1975–76 season, the relegated trio were replaced by Manchester United, Aston Villa and Norwich City, the Mancunian team finishing their Division Two campaign with a 4–0 home win over Blackpool, a result which confirmed them as champions by the comfortable margin of five points. In terms of goalscoring, although Newcastle United finished the season in 15th place, Malcolm Macdonald emerged as the First Division's top scorer with a tally of 21 – the Magpies' striker having also enhanced his growing reputation with a five-goal blast for England against Cyprus at Wembley.

The FA Cup final saw West Ham take on their London rivals Fulham. The game proved to be a bittersweet experience for Bobby Moore. Elated at guiding the Second Division side to the hallowed turf of Wembley – the scene of his greatest moment – he saw the Hammers, his beloved former club, gain an easy 2–0 victory. West Ham therefore returned to the Cup-Winners' Cup in 1975–76, the competition they had won at the end of the 1965 season. In the European Cup, meanwhile, Leeds, after overcoming Barcelona on aggregate, were defeated 2–0 by Bayern Munich in the final in Paris.

For all the excitement that the campaign had produced, it

was sadly remembered as much for the problems on the terraces as for the football. In fact, just as the opening day had been blighted by violence at Orient, the Leeds game in France on 28 May which concluded the season was also the stage for a riot between the rival fans, the Yorkshire supporters instigating fighting after a Peter Lorimer goal had been disallowed.

Division One – final standings 1974–75

		P	W	D	L	GF	GA	PTS
1	**Derby County**	**42**	**21**	**11**	**10**	**67**	**49**	**53**
2	Liverpool	42	20	11	11	60	39	51
3	Ipswich Town	42	23	5	14	66	44	51
4	Everton	42	16	18	8	56	42	50
5	Stoke	42	17	15	10	64	48	49
6	Sheffield United	42	18	13	11	58	51	49
7	Middlesbrough	42	18	12	12	54	40	48
8	Manchester City	42	18	10	14	54	54	46
9	Leeds United	42	16	13	13	57	49	45
10	Burnley	42	17	11	14	68	67	45
11	Queen's Park Rangers	42	16	10	16	54	54	42
12	Wolverhampton Wdrs	42	14	11	17	57	54	39
13	West Ham United	42	13	13	16	58	59	39
14	Coventry City	42	12	15	15	51	62	39
15	Newcastle United	42	15	9	18	59	72	39
16	Arsenal	42	13	11	18	47	49	37
17	Birmingham City	42	14	9	19	53	61	37
18	Leicester City	42	12	12	18	46	60	36
19	Tottenham Hotspur	42	13	8	21	52	63	34
20	Luton Town	42	11	11	20	47	65	33R
21	Chelsea	42	9	15	18	42	72	33R
22	Carlisle United	42	12	5	25	43	59	29R

The celebratory civic procession through Derby to the Council House. The town was getting used to these. Work is in progress on the Assembly Rooms, still well over two years before it finally opened.

EPILOGUE

Champions!

Although the Rams' final points total of 53 was the lowest accumulated by any title-holders since Chelsea had won the League in 1955, many professionals within the game recognised that the championship outcome was in fact a triumph for devotees of the attacking game. Dave Mackay, of course, had been a vital part of the marvellous Tottenham Hotspur side of the 1960s, a team that won a succession of trophies by playing almost perfect football. On departing the Baseball Ground as a player, the mixture of flair and adventure that had been *de rigueur* at White Hart Lane had been duly carried over into his management career. However, for all of the accolades that he gained as a player – being widely remembered as a genuine 'Footballing Legend' – Mackay had no doubts about the value of what his side had achieved in his first full season as the Rams manager. Speaking within moments of hearing that Ipswich Town had failed to beat Manchester City he revealed:

'I had some great moments in my career as a player, but this beats everything. There is something particularly satisfying about winning something as a manager after a long playing career. I always believed we had the players to win the title,

KEVIN HECTOR

ARCHIE GEMMILL

and I never stopped believing we would do it. We tried to do it our way, and that meant playing attacking, entertaining football. It is one thing to win a title, and it is even better to do it in a way which entertains the fans. The Derby players are a great bunch and this season has been a terrific team effort. They have always played the way I wanted to play, and any misunderstandings or bad feelings of the past had disappeared long before we started this season. We have pulled together.'

The jubilant Scot also acknowledged the contribution that Brian Clough had made to the successful Rams team. 'Of course Brian left me with some very good players, but I have also added my own and changed a few things.'

On the subject of his signings, all three of Mackay's major transfers – Bruce Rioch, Francis Lee and Rod Thomas – enjoyed tremendous campaigns. With an overall tally of 20 goals, Rioch had been a revelation, his total astonishing for a midfield player. The reason that the former Aston Villa player was able to get forward on such a regular basis owed a great deal to his two colleagues in the middle of the pitch: Archie Gemmill, who, week in week out, had covered almost every blade of grass, and the less noticeable but superbly effective Henry Newton, who took on the role of the anchor man in front of the defence. At their best the trio were superior to any other midfield unit in the country, and were central to the triumph. Lee brought experience, ability and enthusiasm to the front line, and in accumulating 16 goals he also ensured that Manchester City would eternally regret allowing him to leave Maine Road. The goals of Rioch and Lee complemented each other perfectly, the midfielder relishing the opportunity to produce the spectacular, while Franny's ability to turn a close-range half chance into the net demonstrated that his predatory instinct remained as strong as ever. Of the other strikers, Kevin Hector contributed 21 overall and finished as the Rams' top scorer again – amazingly his consistency being such that

1975 was the ninth consecutive Baseball Ground season that he had recorded an overall tally of at least a dozen goals, the latest batch taking his Derby County total to 168 in 428 appearances, or, put another way – a goal every 2.55 games. Roger Davies responded to his critics with a late season flurry which took his total to 12, and both Alan Hinton and Jeff Bourne, although not regulars throughout the campaign, were effective when required. Hinton was particularly useful in the latter part of the season when teams increasingly arrived at the Baseball Ground happy to defend in the hope of snatching a draw.

In analysing the Rams' defence, while Colin Todd, with his impeccable speed and timing, undoubtably deserved to be named as the PFA 'Footballer of the Year' after an exceptional campaign, Peter Daniel's role in the side should not be underestimated. The fact that the supporters voted him as their player of the season was, according to Roy McFarland, 'a lovely moment.' Gemmill also paid a warm tribute to the Ripley-born defender. 'Peter had a tremendous season, and was a lot better player than what people gave him credit for.' The right-back position was effectively shared between Thomas and Ron Webster, both players appearing in at least 20 league games – although to Webster's credit, Mackay's £80,000 signing from Swindon Town only forced himself into the reckoning after injury had interrupted the veteran defender's season. In their own way, both men brought calmness and a steadying influence to the job, the very characteristic that David Nish delivered in spades on the other side of the back four. Another player who made a vital contribution, despite making only 12 league appearances, was Steve Powell, who demonstrated superb versatility by filling in either in defence or midfeld. Like his father Tommy, Powell went on to be a great servant to the club in the years that followed, the pair between them accumulating in excess of 800 appearances. Although McFarland only played in four games, he returned to the side looking like a player who had been absent for 11 days rather than 11 months. The fact that the Rams did not concede a goal during the quartet of games he appeared in only partly reflected the attributes the England centre-half offered to the club. Behind the defence Colin Boulton, as well as becoming the goalkeeper with the most appearances for the club, regularly showed what a solid performer he was. Like most goalkeepers, he went through a difficult spell during the season, but responded tremendously well when Mackay refused to replace him at the end of October – and along with Rioch he was the only ever-present in the team throughout the 54-game campaign.

The summer brought a game at Wembley for the Rams in the form of the FA Charity Shield against West Ham United. FA Cup

West Ham were the Rams' opponents in the Charity Shield, a game largely regarded by the media of the day as a showpiece between two of the most attractive sides in the country. The Rams beat the FA Cup-winners 2–0 with goals by Hector and this is the second from McFarland, back on the pitch where his career nearly ended. John McDowell wears number two for the Hammers and Mervyn Day is the beaten goalkeeper. Two substitutes were permitted as a trial for the game (only one was allowed in League and Cup matches until as late as 1987–88). West Ham used both theirs. Interestingly, on a baking hot day in what was essentially a friendly, Derby County used neither. Consistency was a key factor in Mackay's successful team. No token run-outs and no savouring the day in those times!

conquerors of Second Division Fulham. (Getting to Wembley was, however, enough to see Fulham's Alan Mullery chosen as Footballer of the Year, rather than a member of the Championship–winning side!). The two attractive teams met on a hot August day.

The Rams, backed by a large following in a crowd of 59,000, started the brighter and went ahead after 20 minutes. Debutant Charlie George found Hector with a superb ball and the Derby striker shot past Day into the far corner.

The Hammers hit back with Pat Holland grazing the bar and Boulton saving well from Jennings, but just before the interval Derby doubled their lead. Lee headed a Nish corner to Hector and his backheel rebounded off Day for Roy McFarland to smash home the loose ball in a fitting Wembley return. Rioch had a goal disallowed and Lee hit the post. All in all it was a great performance, both sides showing all that was good in the game. The Rams were tipped as favourites to retain their title after the 1975–76 campaign.

Derby County: Boulton, Thomas, Nish, Rioch, McFarland, Todd, Newton, Gemmill, Lee, Hector, George. Subs: Unused

West Ham United: Day, McDowell, Lampard, Holland, Taylor (T), Lock, Taylor (A), Paddon, Jennings (Coleman), Brooking, Gould (Robson).

Referee: G.C. Kew (Amsterdam)
Attendance: 59,000

Roy McFarland, back as captain after Gemmill's super season standing in for him, lifts the Charity Shield. Boulton and Rioch look shattered.

Roy McFarland and Archie Gemmill parade the Shield around Wembley.

The following season, although the Rams exited both the European and League Cups at an early stage, they were again strong title contenders, and also enjoyed an extended run in the FA Cup. With seven league fixtures remaining they were in fourth place, just two points behind the surprise leaders Queen's Park Rangers – but significantly with a game in hand. The Rams' position at the time was due largely to the 16 goals of Charlie George, signed by Mackay from Arsenal for just £100,000 – and another marvellous example of the manager's eye for a bargain. The former idol of the North Bank at Highbury responded superbly to Mackay's handling and in addition to his league tally, had also netted eight cup goals; including, most memorably, a hat-trick in the 4–1 home defeat of Real Madrid in the European Cup.

Disaster struck, however, and George dislocated his shoulder in a 2–1 defeat by Stoke City on 24 March 1976 and missed the remainder of the campaign. Without him Derby won just two of their remaining games and were also beaten 2–0 by Manchester United in the semi-final of the FA Cup. Although they hung on to that fourth place the outcome was, as Archie Gemmill recalled, a major disappointment to all concerned:

> 'We were going like steam trains up to Charlie getting injured. We felt within the club that he was most certainly a major loss. We feel to this day, well I do, and I think most of the lads feel the same – if Charlie had stayed fit we could quite easily have done the double. We would definitely have won the league, we were certainly good enough and Charlie was playing out of his skin.'

It was not to be, and after a poor start to the following season Mackay was forced to ask the directors for a vote of confidence. The board did not feel able to give any such assurance, and Mackay and Des Anderson were sacked, the club thus gaining the rather dubious distinction of twice losing its manager within 18 months of winning the championship.

Mackay's departure ended the Rams' reign as one of the country's top teams. Colin Murphy, Tommy Docherty and Colin Addison all attempted to repeat the magical years of Messrs Clough and Mackay but, after several mediocre years, the club was relegated to the Second Division at the end of the 1979–80 campaign. Worse was to follow, and by the start of the 1984–85 season the Rams were in the Third Division and playing in front of crowds of around 12,000. Fortunately, in the summer of 1984 a white knight by the name of Arthur Cox arrived from Newcastle United. With McFarland as his assistant, the reversal in fortunes was well and truly halted. Consecutive promotions followed, the second as Division Two champions, and the Rams commenced their 1987–88 campaign back in the First Division.

Although the details of those years and those since, with Premiership heights and relegation lows both experienced, are beyond the scope of this book, suffice to say there was enough drama and incident within them to complete several more volumes of what was, and indeed continues to be, the remarkable story of Derby County Football Club.

BRUCE RIOCH

ROGER DAVIES

Appendices

APPEARANCES: SEASON 1974–75

PLAYER	LEAGUE	FA CUP	LGE CUP	EUROPE	TOTAL
BOULTON	42	4	2	6	54
WEBSTER	24	2	2	6	34
NISH	38	4	2	5	49
RIOCH	42	4	2	6	54
DANIEL	37	4	2	6	49
TODD	39	4	2	5	50
POWELL	12 *3*	1	1	1	15 *3*
GEMMILL	41	3	2	6	52
DAVIES	39 *1*	3 *1*	2	2 *1*	46 *3*
HECTOR	38	2	2	6	48
LEE	34	4	2	6	46
BOURNE	7 *10*	3 *1*	0 *1*	4 *1*	14 *13*
NEWTON	35 *1*	4	1 *1*	6	46 *2*
THOMAS	22	2	0	1	25
HINTON	8 *5*	0 *2*	0	0 *4*	8 *11*
McFARLAND	4	0	0	0	4
TOTAL	42	4	2	6	54

NB Substitute appearances shown in italics.

GOALSCORERS: SEASON 1974–75

PLAYER	LEAGUE	FA CUP	LGE CUP	EUROPE	TOTAL
HECTOR	13	1	2	5	21
RIOCH	15	2	1	2	20
LEE	12	1	1	2	16
DAVIES	12	0	0	0	12
DANIEL	3	0	0	1	4
BOURNE	2	0	0	2	4
NEWTON	3	0	0	0	3
NISH	2	0	0	1	3
HINTON	2	0	0	1	3
POWELL	2	0	0	0	2
TODD	0	2	0	0	2
WEBSTER	1	0	0	0	1
OWN GOALS	0	0	1	0	1
TOTAL	**67**	**6**	**5**	**14**	**92**

RESULTS SCHEDULE 1974–75

LEAGUE DIVISION ONE

Date		Opposition	Venue	Result	Scorers
August	17	Everton	A	0–0	
	21	**Coventry**	**H**	**1–1**	Lee
	24	**Sheffield Utd**	**H**	**2–0**	Davies, Hector
	27	Coventry	A	1–1	Davies
	31	Tottenham	A	0–2	
September	**7**	**Newcastle**	**H**	**2–2**	Davies, Lee
	14	Birmingham	A	2–3	Rioch, Davies
	21	**Burnley**	**H**	**3–2**	Rioch (P), Hector, Lee
	25	**Chelsea**	**H**	**4–1**	Webster, Rioch, Daniel, Lee
	28	Stoke	A	1–1	Lee
October	5	West Ham	A	2–2	Hector, Lee
	12	**Leicester**	**H**	**1–0**	Rioch
	15	Sheffield Utd	A	2–1	Lee 2
	19	Carlisle	A	0–3	
	26	**Middlesbrough**	**H**	**2–3**	Hector, Hinton
November	2	Leeds	A	1–0	Lee
	9	**Queen's Park R**	**H**	**5–2**	Hector 3, Lee, Rioch
	16	Arsenal	A	1–3	Rioch (P)
	23	**Ipswich**	**H**	**2–0**	Rioch, Hector
December	7	Liverpool	A	2–2	Davies, Bourne
	14	**Everton**	**H**	**0–1**	
	21	Luton	A	0–1	
	26	**Birmingham**	**H**	**2–1**	Rioch, Bourne
	28	Manchester C	A	2–1	Lee, Newton
January	**11**	**Liverpool**	**H**	**2–0**	Lee, Newton
	18	Wolverhampton W	A	0–1	
February	1	Queen's Park R	A	1–4	Rioch
	8	**Leeds**	**H**	**0–0**	
	22	**Arsenal**	**H**	**2–1**	Powell 2
	25	Ipswich	A	0–3	
March	**1**	**Tottenham**	**H**	**3–1**	Rioch, Daniel, Davies
	8	Chelsea	A	2–1	Daniel, Hinton
	15	**Stoke**	**H**	**1–2**	Hector
	22	Newcastle	A	2–0	Nish, Rioch
	29	**Luton**	**H**	**5–0**	Davies 5
	31	Burnley	A	5–2	Hector 2, Davies, Nish, Rioch
April	**1**	**Manchester C**	**H**	**2–1**	Rioch 2
	5	Middlesbrough	A	1–1	Hector
	9	**Wolverhampton W**	**H**	**1–0**	Lee
	12	**West Ham**	**H**	**1–0**	Rioch
	19	Leicester	A	0–0	
	26	**Carlisle**	**H**	**0–0**	

ROY McFARLAND

Bibliography

Derby County A Complete Record 1884–1988, Gerald Mortimer, Breedon Books, 1988.

The Legends of Derby County, Ian Hall, Breedon Books, 2001.

Derby County FC – The 25 Year Record, Michael Robinson, Soccer Book Publishing, 1995.

Cloughie Walking on Water – My Life, John Sadler, Headline Book Publishing, 2002.

Voices of the Rams, Ian Hall, Breedon Books, 2000.

Armed with a Football, Andrew Ward, Crowberry, 1994.

Clough: The Autobiography, John Sadler, Partridge Press, 1996.

His Way – The Brian Clough Story, Patrick Murphy, Pan Books, 1994.

Football Players' Records 1946–1984, Barry Hugman, Newnes Books, 1994.

1888–1988 League Football and the Men who Made It, Simon Inglis, Willow Books, 1988.

The Guinness Football Encyclopedia, Graham Hart, Guinness Publishing, 1995.

Purnell's Encyclopedia of Association Football, Norman Barnett, Purnell Books, 1972.

The Football Managers, Johnny Rogan, Queen Anne Press, 1989.

Shanks – The Authorised Biography of Bill Shankly, Dave Bowler, Orion, 1996.

Jack Charlton, The Autobiography, Partridge Press, 1996.

Various newspapers from the period:

Derby Evening Telegraph

The Times

The Telegraph

The Guardian

For inspiration:

McIlvanney on Football, Hugh McIlvanney, Mainstream Publishing, 1997.

ND - #0264 - 270225 - C0 - 234/156/15 - PB - 9781780914602 - Gloss Lamination